**Development Leads ·** Rob McCreary and
  Owen K.C. Stephens
**Authors ·** Robert Brookes, Liz Courts, Mikko Kallio,
  Jeffrey Swank, and Larry Wilhelm
**Cover Artist ·** Diego Gisbert Llorens
**Interior Artists ·** Tomasz Chistowski, Yan Kyohara,
  Nikolai Ostertag, Roberto Pitturru, and
  Maichol Quinto

**Editor-in-Chief ·** F. Wesley Schneider
**Creative Director ·** James Jacobs
**Creative Design Director ·** Sarah E. Robinson
**Executive Editor ·** James L. Sutter
**Senior Developer ·** Rob McCreary
**Pathfinder Society Lead Developer ·** John Compton
**Developers ·** Adam Daigle, Crystal Frasier,
  Amanda Hamon Kunz, Mark Moreland,
  Owen K.C. Stephens, and Linda Zayas-Palmer
**Managing Editor ·** Judy Bauer
**Senior Editor ·** Christopher Carey
**Editors ·** Jason Keeley, Elisa Mader, and Josh Vogt
**Lead Designer ·** Jason Bulmahn
**Designers ·** Logan Bonner, Stephen Radney-MacFarland,
  and Mark Seifter
**Art Director ·** Sonja Morris
**Senior Graphic Designers ·** Emily Crowell and Adam Vick

**Publisher ·** Erik Mona
**Paizo CEO ·** Lisa Stevens
**Chief Operations Officer ·** Jeffrey Alvarez
**Director of Sales ·** Pierce Watters
**Sales Associate ·** Cosmo Eisele
**Marketing Director ·** Jenny Bendel
**Chief Financial Officer ·** John Parrish
**Staff Accountant ·** Ashley Kaprielian
**Data Entry Clerk ·** B. Scott Keim
**Chief Technical Officer ·** Vic Wertz
**Software Development Manager ·** Cort Odekirk
**Senior Software Developer ·** Gary Teter
**Project Manager ·** Jessica Price
**Organized Play Coordinator ·** Tonya Woldridge
**Adventure Card Game Designer ·** Tanis O'Connor

**Community Team ·** Liz Courts and Chris Lambertz
**Customer Service Team ·** Sharaya Copas, Katina Davis,
  Sara Marie Teter, and Diego Valdez
**Warehouse Team ·** Laura Wilkes Carey, Will Chase,
  Mika Hawkins, Heather Payne, Jeff Strand, and
  Kevin Underwood
**Website Team ·** Christopher Anthony, William Ellis,
  Lissa Guillet, Don Hayes, Julie Iaccarino, and Erik Keith

## ON THE COVER

Kyra and Seelah challenge a glabrezu intruding on the House of Dawn's Redemption in Diego Gisbert Llorens's exciting cover, learning that even a temple to the god of healing isn't always a safe haven.

# TABLE OF CONTENTS

## REFERENCE

This book refers to several Pathfinder Roleplaying Game products using the following abbreviations, yet these additional supplements are not required to make use of this book. Readers interested in references to Pathfinder RPG hardcovers can find the complete rules of these books available online for free at **paizo.com/prd**.

| | | | |
|---|---|---|---|
| *Advanced Class Guide* | ACG | *Monster Codex* | MC |
| *Advanced Player's Guide* | APG | *Ultimate Combat* | UC |
| *Bestiary 2* | B2 | *Ultimate Equipment* | UE |
| *Bestiary 3* | B3 | *Ultimate Magic* | UM |

**paizo®**

Paizo Inc.
7120 185th Ave NE, Ste 120
Redmond, WA 98052-0577

**paizo.com**

# SACRED SPACES AND PROFANE PLACES

Faith is a matter of great import to the people of Golarion. Beyond the 20 gods and goddesses most widely worshiped in the Inner Sea region, scores of archdevils, demon lords, empyreal lords, and other powerful beings are venerated by a wide variety of races and cultures. All of these deities have their own unique temples, bastions of the faith where worshipers can meet with like-minded individuals and pay homage to their chosen focus of obeisance. Adventurers visit these temples as well, often in search of healing, information, spellcasting services, or evil cultists to battle.

This book presents six of the Inner Sea region's most iconic and evocative cathedrals, churches, and temples, from the forests of Kyonin to night-shrouded Nidal, to the sunbaked sands of Osirion. Each section includes a brief overview of the temple, its history, the organization of its priesthood, the composition of its clergy, and the church's relations with other organizations and faiths, as well as a full stat block for at least one of the temple's most notable denizens and a detailed gazetteer and map. The gazetteers are laid out in the same way as full adventures, and are designed so that GMs can run them as is with little preparation or extra work. Finally, each temple includes a section of new rules elements, detailing magic items, spells, occult rituals, or mundane equipment that can be found within the temple or are common among members of the temple's faith.

Obviously, the details presented for the temples in this book are by no means exhaustive—an entire volume could be written on any one of these locations! Rather, the descriptions, sample denizens, and encounter locations described herein are meant to inspire GMs and provide a good starting point for those hoping to run adventures that take place inside a temple dedicated to one of Golarion's major deities. For those who simply want to take a temple layout and modify it to suit the needs of their own campaigns, the maps can easily be extracted for just this purpose; the stat blocks are similarly easy to employ in any campaign at a moment's notice.

## TEMPLE PRIESTS

The priests who reside in the Inner Sea region's numerous temples embody a diverse variety of character classes with a wide array of levels. However, with just a few minor adjustments, you can use the following stat block to represent a typical low- to mid-level cleric whom the player characters might meet at virtually any temple. This stat block is also used for the rank-and-file priests commonly encountered at the six temples described in this book. Each temple section includes a sidebar detailing what changes to make to the standard temple priest stat block below to create a customized priest for that temple and its associated deity.

| TEMPLE PRIEST | CR 4 |
|---|---|

**XP 1,200**
Human cleric 5
N Medium humanoid (human)
**Init** +0; **Senses** Perception +3

---

**DEFENSE**

**AC** 17, touch 10, flat-footed 17 (+7 armor)
**hp** 31 (5d8+5)
**Fort** +4, **Ref** +3, **Will** +7

---

**OFFENSE**

**Speed** 20 ft.
**Melee** mwk heavy mace +5 (1d8+1)
**Ranged** mwk light crossbow +4 (1d8/19–20)
**Special Attacks** channel positive energy 7/day (DC 14, 3d6)
**Domain Spell-Like Abilities** (CL 5th; concentration +8)
  6/day—gentle rest, rebuke death (1d4+2)
**Cleric Spells Prepared** (CL 5th; concentration +8)
  3rd—remove curse, remove disease, speak with dead[D] (DC 16)
  2nd—delay poison, gentle repose[D], remove paralysis, lesser restoration
  1st—bless, bless water, deathwatch[D], magic weapon, sanctuary (DC 14)
  0 (at will)—detect magic, guidance, purify food and drink, stabilize
  **D** domain spell; **Domains** Healing, Repose

---

**STATISTICS**

**Str** 12, **Dex** 10, **Con** 10, **Int** 13, **Wis** 16, **Cha** 14
**Base Atk** +3; **CMB** +4; **CMD** 14
**Feats** Combat Expertise, Extra Channel, Lightning Reflexes, Skill Focus (Heal)
**Skills** Diplomacy +10, Heal +16, Knowledge (religion) +9, Sense Motive +8, Spellcraft +7
**Languages** Celestial, Common
**Combat Gear** scroll of dispel magic, scroll of resist energy, wand of cure light wounds (50 charges), holy water (2); **Other Gear** +1 breastplate, mwk heavy mace, mwk light crossbow with 10 bolts, cleric's vestments, healer's kit, silver holy symbol, spell component pouch, powdered silver (5 lbs. worth 25 gp), 17 gp

## TEMPLE TERMINOLOGY

Religious architecture makes use of a variety of specific terms, and while the average reader can likely distinguish between a cathedral and a crypt, knowing the difference between a narthex and a nave might be more difficult. The following list presents commonly used terms to help readers navigate such jargon.

**Abbey:** A church or residence occupied by the members of a monastic order. An abbey can be a single building or a collection of structures.

**Aisle:** A walkway that runs along the side or down the middle of the central space of a church. Most churches have at least two aisles, one on each side of the nave, which are often delineated by a row of columns or pillars.

**Altar:** A table or block, usually with a flat top, that serves as the focus for religious services, ceremonies, or sacrifices. A temple's altar is usually located in the sanctuary, and is the main focus of that area.

**Ambulatory:** A curving aisle in the apse that goes behind the altar and connects the side aisles of a temple. The ambulatory may also provide access to chapels radiating off of the apse.

**Apse:** A recess at the far end of a temple, often semicircular and capped with a dome. The altar is sometimes placed in the apse, in which case the apse forms part of the chancel. An apse is sometimes called an exedra.

**Baptistery:** The part of a church or temple, sometimes its own dedicated chamber, where baptisms are performed, usually containing a baptismal font.

**Basilica:** An oblong or rectangular church, often with a central nave, aisles, and an apse (sometimes at both ends). Individual basilicas might be granted special ceremonial rights by the head of a faith.

**Cathedral:** Officially, a cathedral is a temple that serves as the seat of a high-ranking church official such as a bishop, but particularly large and/or impressive temples are sometimes referred to by this term as well.

**Chancel:** The part of a temple that contains the altar, choir, and sanctuary, the chancel is typically located at one end of the nave and may end at an apse. The chancel area is usually reserved for members of the clergy only, and is often separated from the nave and the congregation by railings or other barriers.

**Chapel:** A small place of worship that is attached to the main body of a larger temple, and often contains a secondary altar. This kind of chapel might be referred to as a side chapel, but ones radiating outward from an apse are called apse chapels or radiating chapels. Chapels can also be freestanding buildings that function as temples or shrines in their own right.

**Choir:** Also spelled quire, this is the part of a temple between the nave and the altar. The choir is usually part of the chancel, and often contains seats or benches for the use of the clergy and the church's ensemble of singers (also called a choir).

**Clerestory:** The upper part of a wall containing windows, above the heads of worshipers and the roofs of the aisles. In a temple, clerestories usually overlook the nave, transept, and choir, providing light and ventilation to the spaces within.

**Cloister:** A covered walkway, usually with a wall on one side, typically found in monasteries as a symbolic barrier between the monks and the outside world.

**Crypt:** An underground chamber or vault beneath a church, used as a tomb for burials, to store sacred relics, or as a chapel.

**Font:** A basin, usually made of stone, containing holy or unholy water. A font with water for baptisms is called a baptismal font, and is situated in a baptistery.

**Gallery:** A room or area that is partitioned from the rest of the temple proper to provide a place for non-worshipers to observe services.

**Minaret:** A tall, slender tower next to or part of a church or temple with a balcony or gallery from which calls to prayer are made. Often capped with onion domes or conical roofs, minarets can be free standing, and are usually taller than their associated churches.

**Narthex:** The entrance area of a church, usually located at the opposite end of the nave from the altar. Traditionally, the narthex, while part of the church building, is not considered part of the sacred space of the temple proper. A narthex is sometimes called an antechamber or porch.

**Nave:** The central area of a church or temple, a nave holds the majority of the congregation during worship services. It is usually a large, open space, and may contain pews or benches for seating. The nave leads toward the altar at the front of the church, and is often flanked by aisles on either side.

**Pulpit:** A raised platform, often enclosed, where priests stand to address their congregations, deliver sermons, and lead prayers. Other names for similar platforms include bema, bimah, and minbar.

**Rectory:** The residence of a priest, often separate from the church or temple building.

**Reliquary:** A container or storage area for sacred relics.

**Sacristy:** A room in a temple where religious objects and vestments are stored. A sacristy and vestry often serve the same function.

**Sanctuary:** While the term sanctuary can refer to any sacred place, a sanctuary within a church generally refers to the holiest part of the temple that contains the altar. Part of the chancel, a sanctuary often takes the form of an elevated platform. In smaller churches, the chancel and sanctuary may be the same area. A sanctuary can also be called a presbytery.

**Transept:** A portion of a temple that is perpendicular to the nave or main body of the church. A transept separates the nave from the chancel, apse, and altar. In cruciform churches, the two arms of the transept are called semitransepts.

**Vestry:** A room in a temple where cleric's vestments are stored, and where priests prepare themselves for worship services. A vestry and sacristy often serve the same function.

# CATHEDRAL OF EXQUISITE AGONY

"'Joymaking? That doesn't sound too bad,' I said nervously to the Kuthite priest accompanying me. The choir began chanting in an unknown language as four priests carried a man onto the altar and attached chains to his body. The chant reached its climax, peaking on a powerful note before ending abruptly.

"The priests' curved blades fell upon the chained man's arms and legs in perfect unison and with surgical precision, and his severed limbs dropped into the hollow eye sockets of the great silver skull. His loud scream lasted for only a few heartbeats before he passed out, but it felt like an eternity."

—Lieutenant Vektris, Chelish attache

The Cathedral of Exquisite Agony is the primary seat of worship for Zon-Kuthon in Pangolais, the shadow-enshrouded capital of Nidal. Every night at midnight, nearly a thousand people gather there to hear the midnight mass and inflict painful wounds on themselves in religious fervor. The priests of the cathedral are masters of pain, but their intimate knowledge of anatomy and magic also makes them capable healers, and anyone wealthy enough can buy their spellcasting services.

A structure of dark gray marble and steel with wedge-shaped columns bulging from its sides, the Cathedral of Exquisite Agony resembles a giant trilobite from a fever-induced nightmare. Besides the domed cathedral proper, the temple incorporates the Bastille of the Lost, a prison for religious dissidents; the Labyrinth of Lamentation, an ever-changing maze that exists on both the Material Plane and the Shadow Plane; and the Sanctums of Suffering, five shrines where the cathedral's priests torture both paying customers and unwilling prisoners.

## HISTORY

The nation of Nidal was founded during the tumultuous times of the Age of Darkness, when Zon-Kuthon offered the human clans of the region his protection in exchange for their absolute obedience. Ever since, the fate of the tormented god and that of Nidal have been inextricably linked. Darkness prevailed day and night in the capital of Pangolais, allowing the Umbral Court's allies from the Shadow Plane to remain in Nidal to protect the lords' right to rule and to offer them their counsel.

When Cheliax invaded the country in 4338 AR, Nidal experienced an era of relative religious freedom. For the first time in thousands of years, the worship of other deities besides Zon-Kuthon was permitted, and moderate Kuthites held sway over the church. The Cathedral of Exquisite Agony was allowed to operate during this time, and became popular among some of the more decadent Chelish officers and nobles who wanted to experience something new and different.

## KUTHITE PRIESTS

The sample temple priest presented on page 2 can be used to represent a rank-and-file priest of the Cathedral of Exquisite Agony by changing the priest's alignment to lawful evil and making the following adjustments to the stat block.

**Melee** mwk spiked chain +5 (2d4+1)

**Special Attacks** channel negative energy 7/day
(DC 14, 3d6)

**Domain Spell-Like Abilities** (CL 5th; concentration +8)
6/day—*bleeding touch* (2 rounds), *touch of darkness*
(2 rds)

**Cleric Spells Prepared** (CL 5th; concentration +8)
3rd—*cure serious wounds*, *deeper darkness*ᴰ,
*remove curse*
2nd—*blindness/deafness*ᴰ (blindness only,
DC 15), *death knell* (DC 15), *lesser restoration*,
*overstimulate* (DC 15; see page 13)
1st—*cause fear*ᴰ (DC 14), *deathwatch*, *magic weapon*,
*sanctuary* (DC 14), *scarify* (DC 14; see page 13)
0 (at will)—*bleed* (DC 13), *guidance*, *stabilize*, *virtue*
**D** domain spell; **Domains** Darkness, Death

**Skills** Heal +16, Knowledge (religion) +9, Profession
(torturer) +11, Sense Motive +8, Spellcraft +7

During the Chelish Civil War, Nidal sided with House Thrune, and as soon as the Umbral Court returned to power, the laws of religious freedom came to a sudden end. The worship of any gods other than Zon-Kuthon has since been brutally suppressed, and the Cathedral of Exquisite Agony has played a central role in organizing inquisitions to find and punish those who would defy Nidal's laws by teaching false religions to the citizens.

## ORGANIZATION

Among the faithful of Zon-Kuthon are three main schools of thought, which roughly correspond to the three alignments available to Kuthite priests. The most popular view is that all pain is deserved, whether as a reward for those worthy of it or a punishment for those violating Nidal's laws. The most moderate Kuthites, however, believe that pain should be a form of pleasure, and that it should be inflicted only upon consenting individuals. A third and more radical opinion held by the most sadistic followers of the faith states that those who have the power to do so are free to inflict pain and anguish on others, and that those who are oppressed should either become stronger through their suffering or perish.

The priests of the Cathedral of Exquisite Agony have a rigid hierarchy where a superior's commands are absolute, and questioning them is a sure way to end up in the Bastille of the Lost. The church has a merit-based hierarchy based on the priests' physique, their capacity to endure (and willingness to inflict) pain, and most importantly, their ability to unlock the secrets of divine magic granted by the Midnight Lord. The most accomplished priests become rectors—leaders responsible for the cathedral's many functions, such as running one of the shrines. The eldest of the rectors is called the hierarch, who presides over the Cathedral of Exquisite Agony and is the official head of the Kuthite church in Nidal.

Living in the perpetual darkness of Pangolais, most priests of the Cathedral of Exquisite Agony are as pale as death, and their gaunt frames are covered in scars. To show their devotion to Zon-Kuthon, some priests undergo even more radical body modifications, such as stretching their necks with silver rings, splitting their tongues, or even having an eye removed. Priests of the Cathedral of Exquisite Agony wear garments of black leather and silver with vertical spikes forming a collar, and often wear clawed rings and dark eye makeup. During services, the priests don even more extravagant vestments that would be inconvenient or dangerous to have on all the time, such as barbed chains attached to their bodies.

## MEMBERSHIP AND RELATIONS

In Nidal, the worship of Zon-Kuthon is the singular religion permitted by law, and for this reason every permanent citizen is subject to the church and required to observe religious doctrine and tradition. In practice, however, most Nidalese venerate Zon-Kuthon only habitually or out of fear. In decadent Pangolais, the very heart of the Kuthite religion, the number of true Kuthites is much higher than in any other part of the country. Devout believers show their dedication to their god through piercings, self-inflicted scars, and other body modifications. Some of the most fervent and wealthiest followers of Zon-Kuthon undergo a ceremony called the Joymaking, where "unnecessary flesh" is removed and their limbs are amputated. These devout individuals, called Joyful Things, are allowed to remain in the church's dark torture chambers until the end of their painful existence.

Because the Umbral Court's shadowy powers come directly from Zon-Kuthon and Nidal's government is established around his worship, the priests of the Cathedral of Exquisite Agony enjoy a privileged position in Pangolais. The cathedral's leaders answer only to the city's ruling council, the Black Triune. The authorities question little of what transpires in the temple, as even the cruelest forms of torture and mutilation are legal. The church's contributions to Nidal's police and military strength are also considerable. Kuthite priests and inquisitors lead some of the country's most prestigious combat units.

While Pangolais is open to visitors, foreigners are carefully supervised to curb any espionage attempts. The only portion of the Cathedral of Exquisite Agony that foreigners can enter without a church-assigned escort is the sacred house of body modifications called the Wounded Flesh.

## NOTABLE DENIZENS

Among the inhabitants of the Cathedral of Exquisite Agony is a Joymade necrocraft, a constructlike undead creature crafted from the disposed body parts of those who undergo the Joymaking ceremony.

---

### JOYMADE NECROCRAFT — CR 7

**XP 3,200**

Unique necrocraft (*Pathfinder RPG Bestiary 4* 200)

NE Huge undead

**Init** –1; **Senses** darkvision 60 ft.; Perception +0

#### DEFENSE

**AC** 20, touch 7, flat-footed 20 (–1 Dex, +13 natural, –2 size)

**hp** 75 (10d8+30)

**Fort** +5, **Ref** +2, **Will** +7

**Immune** undead traits

#### OFFENSE

**Speed** 30 ft.

**Melee** 3 claws +15 (1d8+10)

**Space** 15 ft.; **Reach** 15 ft.

#### STATISTICS

**Str** 31, **Dex** 9, **Con** —, **Int** —, **Wis** 10, **Cha** 14

**Base Atk** +7; **CMB** +19; **CMD** 28

**Feats** Toughness[B]

**SQ** construction points (bone armor [2], cannibalize, extra attack [claw])

---

Rector Shakrenistre oversees the tortures in the shrine.

---

### SHAKRENISTRE — CR 10

**XP 9,600**

Female kyton inquisitor of Zon-Kuthon 7 (*Pathfinder RPG Bestiary* 185, *Pathfinder RPG Advanced Player's Guide* 38)

LE Medium outsider (evil, extraplanar, kyton, lawful)

**Init** +10; **Senses** darkvision 60 ft., *deathwatch*; Perception +16

#### DEFENSE

**AC** 24, touch 16, flat-footed 20 (+4 armor, +2 deflection, +3 Dex, +1 dodge, +4 natural)

**hp** 140 (15 HD; 7d8+8d10+65); regeneration 2 (good weapons and spells, silver weapons)

**Fort** +15, **Ref** +11, **Will** +10

**DR** 5/good or silver; **Immune** cold; **SR** 17

#### OFFENSE

**Speed** 30 ft.

**Melee** *+1 spiked chain* +18/+13/+8 (2d4+7) or 4 chains +18 (2d4+4)

**Space** 5 ft.; **Reach** 5 ft. (10 ft. with chains)

**Special Attacks** bane (7 rounds/day), dancing chains, judgment 3/day, unnerving gaze (DC 16)

**Domain Spell-Like Abilities** (CL 7th; concentration +7)

6/day—*touch of fatigue* (DC 10)

**Inquisitor Spell-Like Abilities** (CL 7th; concentration +10)

At will—*detect alignment, discern lies* (7 rounds/day)

**Inquisitor Spells Known** (CL 7th; concentration +10)

3rd (2/day)—*fester*[APG] (DC 16), *locate weakness*[UC]

2nd (4/day)—*confess*[APG] (DC 15), *delay pain*[UM] (DC 15), *howling agony*[UM] (DC 15), *instrument of agony*[UC]

1st (5/day)—*command* (DC 14), *inflict light wounds* (DC 14), *interrogation*[UM] (DC 14), *persuasive goad*[UM] (DC 14), *scarify* (DC 14; see page 13)

inner sea temples

Sacred Spaces and Profane Places

Cathedral of Exquisite Agony

Cayden's Hall

First Colonial Bank of Sargava

High Temple of Pharasma

House of Dawn's Redemption

Imvrildara

CATHEDRAL OF EXQUISITE AGONY
1 SQUARE = 5 FEET

0 (at will)—*acid splash, bleed* (DC 13), *brand*[APG] (DC 13), *guidance, stabilize, virtue*

**Domain** Torture inquisition[UM]

**STATISTICS**

**Str** 18, **Dex** 17, **Con** 18, **Int** 13, **Wis** 16, **Cha** 10

**Base Atk** +13; **CMB** +17; **CMD** 33

**Feats** Ability Focus (unnerving gaze), Alertness, Blind-Fight, Dodge, Escape Route[UC], Improved Initiative, Insightful Gaze[UM], Merciful Bane[UC], Scarred Legion[MC], Weapon Focus (chains)

**Skills** Acrobatics +14, Climb +15, Craft (blacksmith) +10, Escape Artist +14, Heal +21, Intimidate +25, Knowledge (planes, religion) +10, Perception +16, Profession (torturer) +23, Sense Motive +23

**Languages** Common, Infernal, Shadowtongue

**SQ** chain armor, monster lore +3, solo tactics, stern gaze +3, torturer's touch, track +3

**Gear** *+1 spiked chain, deathwatch eyes*[UE], *ring of protection +2*, mwk torturer's tools, silver holy symbol of Zon-Kuthon, spell component pouch

## GAZETTEER

The Cathedral of Exquisite Agony is located in the central part of Pangolais, near the palace of the Black Triune.

## 1. THE WOUNDED FLESH (CR 4)

This state-sponsored body modification studio is reputedly the best in Nidal (and quite possibly in the entire Inner Sea region), and its list of services is several pages long, including various kinds of branding, grafts, implants, piercings, scarification, tattoos, and removal of non-vital body parts. The prices vary from 5 gp to 500 gp depending on the duration and difficulty of the operation. Because of the establishment's popularity, it can take weeks to get an appointment. The Wounded Flesh also schedules appointments for those customers wishing to partake of the services offered in the cathedral's five Sanctums of Suffering (areas **10** through **14**), where the waiting lists aren't quite as long.

**Creature:** The thoroughly pierced and tattooed Rector Zandira is chief chirurgeon of the Wounded Flesh. She guarantees that any modifications performed here will never cause infection or rejection by the customer's body.

| ZANDIRA | CR 4 |
|---|---|

**XP 1,200**

LE female temple priest (see page 2 and the sidebar on page 6)

**hp** 31

## 2. NAVE

The central nave accommodates the temple's congregation during religious services. Ribbed vaulting supports the ceiling, reaching a height of 60 feet at the apex. Two curving staircases at the south end of the chamber lead up to galleries 30 feet above the floor on either side of the nave. One-inch-thick iron bars separate the nave from the chancel to the north (area **4**). The nave is large enough to hold 1,000 people packed tightly together, with room for 150 more in the galleries.

**Hazard:** During services, the air is alive with the fervent screams of worshipers and the ominous chanting of the choir in the chancel. The packed congregation is considered a crowd (*Pathfinder RPG Core Rulebook* 436), and a creature in a square adjacent to the iron bars at the front of the nave must succeed at a DC 15 Fortitude save every 10 minutes or take 1d6 points of nonlethal damage from the weight of the crowd pushing against it.

## 3. CHAPELS OF JOY

Each of the five small chapels on the west side of the nave houses a single Joyful Thing, a devout worshiper who has dedicated her life to suffering the pleasures of endless torture by having her limbs amputated and all nonessential tissue (eyes, ears, lips, nose, and reproductive organs) removed. These five Joyful Things have been gifted with oracular powers, which awaken in only a few who undergo the procedure, and are constantly spouting dark prophecies that few can understand.

## 4. CHANCEL (CR 7)

The main feature of the cathedral's most sacred space is the altar, a 40-foot-diameter silver skull with chains through its eye sockets, forming a raised platform in the shape of Zon-Kuthon's unholy symbol. A large windlass sits west of the altar to raise or lower the skull platform. Operating the windlass requires a successful DC 20 Strength check. Five elevated platforms for the cathedral's choir are arranged behind the altar. The choir includes both male and female singers, including a few castrati who are envied all across Golarion for their unique voices but also pitied and disparaged for the cruelty they endured to attain them.

**Creature:** The eye sockets of the skull altar are hollow shafts that lead down 30 feet to an underground chamber inhabited by a necrocraft composed of discarded humanoid limbs and corpses. After Joymaking ceremonies atop the altar, the priests dispose of any removed body parts by throwing them down the shafts into the necrocraft's lair, where the creature uses its cannibalize ability to incorporate the parts into its body.

| JOYMADE NECROCRAFT | CR 7 |
|---|---|

**XP 3,200**

**hp** 75 (see page 7)

## 5. SACRISTY

The cathedral's priests prepare themselves for religious services in this room, which contains a table and chairs, a large chest, and three cabinets along the north wall.

inner sea temples

Sacred Spaces and Profane Places

Cathedral of Exquisite Agony

Cayden's Hall

First Colonial Bank of Sargava

High Temple of Pharasma

House of Dawn's Redemption

Imvrildara

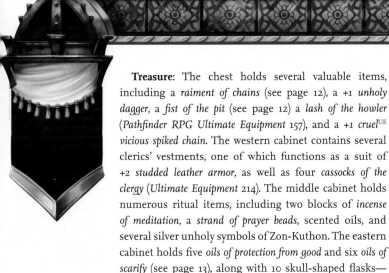

**Treasure:** The chest holds several valuable items, including a *raiment of chains* (see page 12), a *+1 unholy dagger*, a *fist of the pit* (see page 12) a *lash of the howler* (*Pathfinder RPG Ultimate Equipment* 157), and a *+1 cruel*[UE] *vicious spiked chain*. The western cabinet contains several clerics' vestments, one of which functions as a suit of *+2 studded leather armor*, as well as four *cassocks of the clergy* (*Ultimate Equipment* 214). The middle cabinet holds numerous ritual items, including two blocks of *incense of meditation*, a *strand of prayer beads*, scented oils, and several silver unholy symbols of Zon-Kuthon. The eastern cabinet holds five *oils of protection from good* and six *oils of scarify* (see page 13), along with 10 skull-shaped flasks—each with a chain through the eye sockets that can be used as a handle—that contain unholy water.

## 6. Hierarch's Office

The cathedral's high priest, **Hierarch Chartaigne** (LE male vampire cleric of Zon-Kuthon 13) conducts official business here, assigning targets for the church's inquisitors to capture or kill and managing the church's wealth, workforce, and other resources. The pale vampire's skin is branded with verses from Zon-Kuthon's holy text, *Umbral Leaves*. A busy creature, Chartaigne usually spends only a few hours each day in his office. He more often resides in his grand, labyrinthine mansion—one of Pangolais's largest privately owned houses—that resembles a tomb more than it does a residence.

## 7. Gallery of Cages (CR 9)

A plaque on a wall of this chamber reads, "Ten vile enemies of the church."

**Creatures:** The unfortunate people on display here were once leaders of Desnan and other forbidden cults, but they are now undead wights, imprisoned in cages and wrapped in chains and dark leather straitjackets, as if to show that all residing in Nidal are Kuthites whether they like it or not. So bound, the wights have the grappled condition, unable to do anything except suffer eternally unless released from their restraints and freed from their cages (hardness 10, hp 30, break DC 28, Disable Device DC 30).

| WIGHTS (10) | CR 3 |
|---|---|

**XP 800 each**

**hp** 26 each (*Pathfinder RPG Bestiary* 276)

## 8. Labyrinth of Lamentation (CR 10)

Initiates are tested and prisoners are tortured and killed in the winding halls of this maze. Due to repeated castings of the call the darkness occult ritual (see page 12), the Material Plane and Shadow Plane blend together here, and creatures from Zon-Kuthon's domain of Xovaikain can cross over to the Material Plane.

**Creatures:** A cruel, impossibly obese man called the **Lord of Rapture** (LE male giant human inquisitor of Zon-Kuthon 13) presides over the cathedral's Labyrinth of Lamentation. His limbs amputated and his eyes removed, the Lord of Rapture lives in a large cage and is fed through tubes, but he is far from helpless. He has blindsight to a range of 30 feet, and when needed, he grows arachnid limbs of shadowstuff, giving him a climb speed of 40 feet, as his cage bends and twists to release him. The Lord of Rapture also controls the shape and extent of the labyrinth, which modifies itself at his mad whims.

The Veiled Sentinels, a pair of twin svartalfar assassins in featureless white masks, serve the Lord of Rapture. They defend the him and his labyrinth, silently kill any spies or intruders, and capture any prisoners who attempt to escape.

| VEILED SENTINELS (2) | CR 8 |
|---|---|

**XP 4,800 each**

Svartalfar (*Pathfinder RPG Bestiary 4* 256)

**hp** 84 each

## 9. Bastille of the Lost (CR 11)

Enemies of the faith invariably end up in this tower prison within the Cathedral of Exquisite Agony. The five floors of the bastille are nearly identical, with all but the first floor containing 14 bare, windowless cells. Given only scant food and water, prisoners are expected to reflect on their wrongdoings while they wait in their cells in preparation for regular torture and interrogation sessions. These sessions usually take place in the open areas in the center of each floor, though prisoners are sometimes taken to one of the cathedral's five Sanctums of Suffering (areas **10** through **14**) for more thorough torment. The screams of the victims can be heard at almost every hour, night and day. On the rare occasions that a prisoner displays enough cooperation and repentance to be released, the church assigns a handler to monitor the former inmate and extract more information from him as needed.

**Creature:** Rector Armius is in charge of the Bastille of the Lost and all inmates imprisoned within, ably assisted by a sacristan kyton called Brother Dolor.

| RECTOR ARMIUS | CR 6 |
|---|---|

**XP 2,400**

Male vivisectionist cleric (*Pathfinder RPG NPC Codex* 48)

**hp** 56

| BROTHER DOLOR | CR 10 |
|---|---|

**XP 9,600**

Sacristan kyton (*Pathfinder RPG Bestiary 4* 177)

**hp** 126

## 10. The Burning Angel

One of the cathedral's five Sanctums of Suffering, this simple shrine contains only an ancient stone slab with an angel carved into its surface, which continuously heals and regenerates any creature lying on it as per *regenerate*. Customers (or prisoners) are chained to the slab while **Rector Lamentia** (LE female erinyes oracle[APG] 6) and her assistants use acid, alchemist's fire, flaying knives, amputation scissors, and other implements to torture their subjects. She now wears a mechanical wing with razor-sharp steel feathers to replace a wing that was amputated as punishment for failing a mission. Extremely skilled in her trade, Lamentia knows the exact amount of pain a customer can take without dying, and often uses *overstimulate* (see page 13) to keep subjects near death but fully aware of the pain.

## 11. Hope's Tomb (CR varies)

This shrine specializes in tormenting its customers with undead horrors.

**Creatures:** **Rector Sharael** (NE male dhampir[B2] cleric of Zon-Kuthon 10) calls forth controlled undead creatures from a tomb beneath the room, usually ghouls (to paralyze subjects and feed on their flesh) or shadows (to drain subjects' strength with their chilling touches).

| GHOULS (8) | CR 1 |
|---|---|
| **XP 400 each** | |

**hp** 13 each (*Pathfinder RPG Bestiary* 146)

| SHADOWS (4) | CR 3 |
|---|---|
| **XP 800 each** | |

**hp** 19 each (*Pathfinder RPG Bestiary* 245)

## 12. The Carousel

Named for the large, rotating wheel outfitted with long spikes in the center of the chamber, this shrine serves customers wishing to experience the pain of impalement. **Rector Ephrasiet** (NE male fetchling[B2] inquisitor[APG] of Zon-Kuthon 9) and his team take special care to impale their subjects on the spikes through the middle of the torso, carefully avoiding damage to any internal organs. Once the subjects are in place on the Carousel's spikes, the device starts spinning, inflicting great but nonfatal pain upon the impaled victims.

## 13. Feast Hall (CR 8)

Four iron cages are the primary feature of this shrine. **Rector Anehica** (LN female human witch[APG] 9) summons and releases swarms of vermin to feast on the flesh of customers or prisoners locked in the cages. Paying customers can select the specific pests that will feed on their flesh, or they can leave the choice to the shrine's priests. After just a few minutes, the subjects are usually unconscious or comatose from massive poisoning and the pain of thousands of bites, but Anehica and her assistants provide healing and restoration spells before releasing the customers from the shrine.

**Trap:** When the Feast Hall is closed, the shrine is warded by a *creeping doom* trap that summons swarms into the room to attack intruders.

| CREEPING DOOM TRAP | CR 8 |
|---|---|
| **XP 4,800** | |

**Type** magic; **Perception** DC 32; **Disable Device** DC 32

**EFFECTS**

**Trigger** visual (*darkvision*); **Duration** 13 rounds; **Reset** automatic (12 hours); **Bypass** hidden lock **Effect** spell effect (*creeping doom*, summons 4 swarms of insects, DC 20 Fort save partial)

## 14. House of Hooks (CR 10)

Priests skillfully suspend customers from this shrine ceiling with chains affixed to carefully placed metal hooks that pierce the subjects' flesh. The act of suspension inflicts pain and induces an adrenaline rush, but does not usually harm the body severely. Most customers can endure suspension for merely a few minutes, but some spend hours hanging from the hooks, remaining suspended until their own weight tears the bloody barbs out of their flesh.

**Creature:** The kyton inquisitor Rector Shakrenistre oversees the House of Hooks. An adroit torturer, Shakrenistre prefers unwilling victims, but her inherent predilection for sadomasochism enables her to enjoy inflicting pain on eager customers as well as on herself.

| SHAKRENISTRE | CR 10 |
|---|---|
| **XP 9,600** | |

**hp** 140 (see page 7)

SHAKRENISTRE

inner sea temples

Sacred Spaces and Profane Places

Cathedral of Exquisite Agony

Cayden's Hall

First Colonial Bank of Sargava

High Temple of Pharasma

House of Dawn's Redemption

Imvrildara

# KUTHITE MAGIC

The following section details magic items, an occult ritual, and spells favored by priests and followers of Zon-Kuthon.

## KUTHITE MAGIC ITEMS

Priests of the Cathedral of Exquisite Agony often make use of the following magic items.

| FIST OF THE PIT | | PRICE 9,305 GP |
|---|---|---|
| **SLOT** none | **CL** 6th | **WEIGHT** 1 lb. |
| **AURA** moderate conjuration | | |

This *+1 spiked gauntlet* is shaped like a skull studded with metal spikes. Once per day as a standard action, the wearer can strike the ground with the gauntlet, causing a 10-foot-square, 30-foot-deep extradimensional pit filled with spikes to open within 30 feet, as per *spiked pit* (*Pathfinder RPG Advanced Player's Guide* 246). The gauntlet's enhancement bonus is added to the piercing damage caused by the pit's spikes. If the wearer increases the gauntlet's enhancement bonus (such as with *greater magic weapon* or a paladin's divine bond ability), the additional weapon enhancement bonus is also added to the damage. Similarly, if the gauntlet has any weapon special abilities that deal extra damage (such as *flaming* or *wounding*), this extra damage is likewise added to the damage caused by the pit's spikes. Weapon special abilities that don't deal extra damage, or that deal damage to the wielder as well (such as *vicious*) do not affect the pit's spikes.

| CONSTRUCTION REQUIREMENTS | COST 4,805 GP |
|---|---|
| Craft Magic Arms and Armor, *spiked pit*APG | |

| RAIMENT OF CHAINS | | PRICE 6,250 GP |
|---|---|---|
| **SLOT** armor | **CL** 5th | **WEIGHT** 25 lbs. |
| **AURA** faint transmutation | | |

While unattended, this *+1 chain shirt* takes the shape of a heap of rusty chains, but when a creature picks up the armor, the shirt immediately starts to assume its true form. The chains eagerly wrap or willingly loosen around the wearer's body, allowing the wearer to don or remove the armor as a move action. A *raiment of chains* can't be "donned hastily."

Three times per day as a standard action, the wearer can command chains to shoot out from the *raiment of chains* and attempt a reposition or trip combat maneuver check against a single target within 20 feet. The wearer is considered proficient with the chains and uses her own CMB with a +1 enhancement bonus on the check. The combat maneuver provokes attacks of opportunity as normal. The chains immediately retract back into the armor once the combat maneuver check has been attempted.

| CONSTRUCTION REQUIREMENTS | COST 3,250 GP |
|---|---|
| Craft Magic Arms and Armor, animate objects, chain of perditionUC | |

## KUTHITE OCCULT RITUAL

The priests of the Cathedral of Exquisite Agony use the following occult ritual to allow creatures of the Shadow Plane to cross over to the Material Plane. Full rules for occult rituals can be found on pages 208–209 of *Pathfinder RPG Occult Adventures*.

### CALL THE DARKNESS

**School** conjuration (creation or calling); **Level** 9
**Casting Time** 90 minutes
**Components** V, S, M (black diamond dust worth 10,000 gp), SC (at least 8, up to 16)
**Skill Checks** Knowledge (geography) DC 36, 2 successes; Knowledge (planes) DC 36, 3 successes; Knowledge (religion) DC 36, 2 successes; Spellcraft DC 36, 2 successes
**Range** close (25 ft. + 5 ft./character level of the primary caster)
**Effect** up to 20 10-ft. cubes/character level of the primary caster
**Duration** 10 minutes/character level of the primary caster (D); see text
**Saving Throw** none; **Spell Resistance** no
**Backlash** The primary caster takes 1 permanent negative level.
**Failure** All casters must succeed at a Will saving throw (DC = 19 + primary caster's Charisma modifier) or be transported to a random location on the Shadow Plane, as per *plane shift*.

#### EFFECT

This ritual must be cast on the Material Plane. The primary caster begins the ritual by delineating the boundaries of the area to be affected using the black diamond dust. The casters link hands and chant verses from Zon-Kuthon's holy book, *Umbral Leaves*. Upon the ritual's completion, magical darkness fills the designated area as the Material Plane and Shadow Plane blend together there. The affected area thereafter exists simultaneously on both planes, becoming an amalgam of the two. A thin layer of impenetrable darkness surrounds the affected area, so it is impossible to see beyond the area's boundaries into either plane. Colors appear faded in the area, but not completely black and white as on the Shadow Plane. The area has the enhanced magic and impeded magic traits of the Shadow Plane (*Pathfinder RPG GameMastery Guide* 188), but all other planar traits correspond to those of the Material Plane. As long as the primary caster remains within range of the designated area, this effect lasts for up to 10 minutes per character level of the primary caster, but if the primary caster ever moves beyond the range, the effect immediately ends.

Any creature that enters the affected area remains on the same plane as before but can interact with creatures on the other plane as though they were on the same plane. While casting this ritual, the primary caster can set a condition that allows creatures to cross over from the Shadow Plane to the Material Plane or vice versa. This condition can be a password, a specific action that a creature must take (such as stepping through a mirror), or a specific type of item that a creature must carry in order to cross over. Alternatively, the primary caster can grant a creature passage between the two planes as a standard action. If the primary caster does not set a condition or grant passage, creatures cannot cross between the two planes.

## KUTHITE SPELLS

Priests of Zon-Kuthon enjoy inflicting misery upon the devout and others with the following spells.

### BEREAVE

**School** enchantment (compulsion) [mind-affecting]; **Level** bard 3, cleric 4, mesmerist 3, psychic 4, witch 4
**Casting Time** 1 standard action
**Components** V, S, M/DF (a broken chain link)
**Range** medium (100 ft. + 10 ft./level)
**Targets** all creatures in a 15-ft.-radius burst
**Duration** 1 round/level
**Saving Throw** Will negates; **Spell Resistance** yes

An overwhelming feeling of loss overcomes the targets, and their allies' words sound bleak and hollow. Regardless of actual allegiances, affected creatures no longer count as allies for other creatures and always count as enemies for the purposes of abilities, effects, and spells that differentiate between allies and enemies, such as flanking or spells such as *bane* or *bless*. Allies of an affected creature must succeed at a melee touch attack to affect the subject with touch spells, and an affected creature cannot voluntarily fail a saving throw even if the effect is harmless (such as *cure light wounds*). An affected creature still counts as her own ally and can target herself with abilities, effects, and spells normally.

### OVERSTIMULATE

**School** transmutation; **Level** alchemist 2, bard 2, bloodrager 2, cleric 2, druid 2, psychic 2, ranger 2, shaman 2, summoner 2, witch 2
**Casting Time** 1 standard action
**Components** V, S, M/DF (smelling salts)
**Range** close (25 ft. + 5 ft./2 levels)
**Target** one creature
**Duration** 1 round/level
**Saving Throw** Fortitude negates (harmless); **Spell Resistance** yes (harmless)

You deprive a creature of the blissful oblivion of unconsciousness, either to keep it going despite grievous injuries or to prolong its suffering. For the duration of the spell, the target gains the ferocity ability (*Pathfinder RPG Bestiary* 300), allowing it to remain conscious and continue fighting even if its hit point total is below 0. The target is still staggered and loses 1 hit point each round, and the target still dies when its hit point total reaches a negative amount equal to its Constitution score.

### SCARIFY

**School** necromancy; **Level** adept 1, alchemist 1, antipaladin 1, cleric 1, druid 1, inquisitor 1, shaman 1, spiritualist 1, witch 1
**Casting Time** 1 standard action
**Components** V, S
**Range** touch
**Target** creature touched
**Duration** instantaneous
**Saving Throw** Fortitude negates (harmless); **Spell Resistance** yes (harmless)

Your touch causes a single creature's skin to produce fibrous tissue that sutures the creature's wounds, rapidly closing them and leaving jagged scars where the wounds were. The process is painful, and converts 2d6 points of damage + 1 point per caster level (maximum +5) into nonlethal damage. If the target creature is immune to nonlethal damage, the spell fails. Damage resistance against nonlethal damage reduces the amount of damage converted. This effect counts as healing for the purpose of stopping bleed damage. Kuthites are especially fond of this spell, as it gives them permanent physical reminders of the all too brief pain they endured.

### SHROUD OF DARKNESS

**School** evocation [darkness]; **Level** antipaladin 4, bard 5, cleric 5, inquisitor 5, mesmerist 4, shaman 5, sorcerer/wizard 5
**Casting Time** 1 standard action
**Components** V, S, M/DF (a pinch of black sand)
**Range** medium (100 ft. + 10 ft./level)
**Targets** one creature/3 levels, no two of which can be more than 30 ft. apart
**Duration** 1 round/level (D)
**Saving Throw** Will negates; **Spell Resistance** yes

With a dark incantation and a gesture of your hand over your eyes, you cause a shroud of darkness to descend upon the targets of this spell. The subjects treat the light level as two steps lower than normal for the duration of this spell. Bright light becomes dim light, normal light becomes darkness, and areas of dim light and darkness become supernaturally dark (as *darkness*, but even creatures with darkvision cannot see).

inner sea temples

Sacred Spaces and Profane Places

Cathedral of Exquisite Agony

Cayden's Hall

First Colonial Bank of Sargava

High Temple of Pharasma

House of Dawn's Redemption

Imvrildara

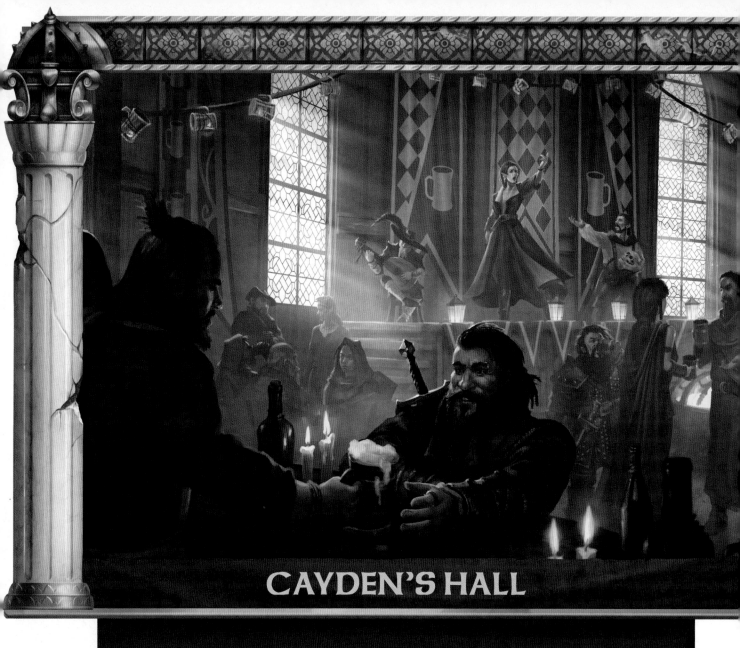

# CAYDEN'S HALL

Good crowd tonight. A new band of adventurers staggered in during Midnight Mead, including a half-orc infected with something nasty. I would normally charge to remove an infection... but I've seen wrist scars like hers before. The charity made her suspicious, but by the time she proved her boast about Five Barrels and a Mule she seemed very much at home. She also spent many long minutes staring at the big Placard of Wisdom over the entrance. If she and her friends come back soon, I think I'll ask if they'd like to do me a favor and check out the reports of missing children in Puddles.

—From Cayden's Hall Holy Journal and
Official Bar Tab, High Priestess Saphira

Located in the Ascendant Court district of Absalom, Cayden's Hall is the most famous of all temples to Cayden Cailean and is supposedly the last tavern the Accidental God caroused at before taking the drunken dare that set him on a course to divinity. Even though the building has burned to the ground and been rebuilt more than a dozen times over the ensuing centuries, the Drunken Hero's faithful still consider the current Cayden's Hall to be the original. Cayden's Hall functions as the premiere center of Cayden Cailean's worship—as well as a popular alehouse and gathering place for all lovers of freedom, adventure, and alcoholic spirits (not necessarily in that order).

## HISTORY

In the nearly 2,000 years since Cayden Cailean attained divinity, the mead hall on this site has burned down 16 times, most recently just a few years ago following the popularity of a flammable drink that has since been removed from the menu. Long tradition demands that Cayden's Hall continue to be made out of wood, as it was when Cayden Cailean was mortal, and that still holds true to this day, despite the obvious disadvantages. Given the consequences when drink and fire are involved, the most recent reconstruction included the addition of several stone pillars to aid in the inevitable reconstruction of Cayden's Hall.

## ORGANIZATION

The church of Cayden Cailean has no real hierarchy; much like the god himself, the church's priests value personal freedoms too much to order anybody around, especially each other. Without even a standardized system of titles among the clergy, each center of Cayden Cailean's worship uses its own ranks. At Cayden's Hall, the head of the small congregation of Caydenite faithful is referred to as the high priest or priestess, with the assistants going by acolyte, brother, or sister. High Priestess Saphira rarely goes by her official title, instead preferring "Sister," when she uses a title at all. The title of high priestess is bestowed by the

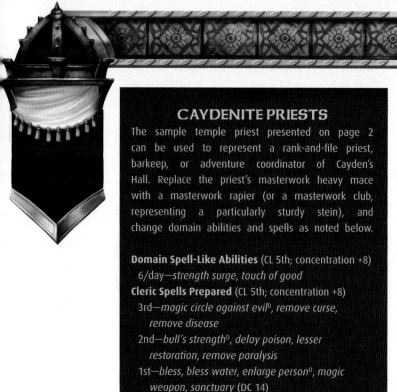

## CAYDENITE PRIESTS

The sample temple priest presented on page 2 can be used to represent a rank-and-file priest, barkeep, or adventure coordinator of Cayden's Hall. Replace the priest's masterwork heavy mace with a masterwork rapier (or a masterwork club, representing a particularly sturdy stein), and change domain abilities and spells as noted below.

**Domain Spell-Like Abilities** (CL 5th; concentration +8)
6/day—*strength surge, touch of good*
**Cleric Spells Prepared** (CL 5th; concentration +8)
3rd—*magic circle against evil*[D], *remove curse, remove disease*
2nd—*bull's strength*[D], *delay poison, lesser restoration, remove paralysis*
1st—*bless, bless water, enlarge person*[D], *magic weapon, sanctuary* (DC 14)
0 (at will)—*detect magic, guidance, purify food and drink, stabilize*
**D** domain spell; **Domains** Good, Strength

priests who have the most seniority rather than candidates undergoing grueling rites of fasting and prayer.

Characters who wish to join the ranks of Cayden Cailean's clergy are not expected to remember long litanies of prayers or dress themselves in a particular way, and they are certainly not expected to deny themselves the pleasures of the flesh. They are simply expected to consider *The Placard of Wisdom*, Cayden Cailean's sole holy book, and prove themselves dedicated to the cause of the church.

## MEMBERSHIP AND RELATIONS

In Cayden's Hall, it is hard to distinguish the clergy from the revelers. The faith is as diverse as Absalom itself and reflects the cosmopolitan nature of the city. Half-orcs and other cross-blooded races find themselves welcome here. Gender and race discrimination among the congregation here is nearly unheard of (and examples of it among new attendees are not tolerated).

Joining the church is not difficult. Expressing the desire to help others be free to make their own choices and enjoy life to the fullest is enough to convince High Priestess Saphira to allow someone to become an initiate. However, this is not a free pass to an easy lifestyle in the priesthood; Saphira usually insists that applicants assist her in numerous ways, including serving drinks, running errands, and cleaning up each morning.

Adventurers are fond of Cayden Cailean's church, and the feeling is often mutual. If an individual or group does a major service for the church, or simply impresses or amuses Saphira to a very high degree, she names them "honored guests," making note of it in her official journal, allowing them to eat, drink, and even sleep by the hearth at Cayden's Hall free of charge.

Relations with other holy institutions in Absalom are cordial for the most part. Followers of Shelyn are most welcome, and Desnans' love of travel often brings rare and unusual spirits to Cayden's Hall. Followers of the dwarven god Torag know they can get a good drink here, and devotees of the Dawnflower know that if there is a just cause to fight for in Absalom, there is always a member of Cayden Cailean's faithful willing to offer her sword arm in assistance. However, Asmodeans are not encouraged to drink in Cayden's Hall, though it isn't forbidden outright.

## NOTABLE DENIZENS

While nearly any NPC might be present at Cayden's Hall on a given night, there are a few major characters who are present most of the time.

| EGGAL TORKELSON | CR 5 |
|---|---|

**XP 1,600**

Male halfling cleric of Cayden Cailean 6 (*Pathfinder NPC Codex* 47)

**hp** 54

A well-known local, Eggal is an honored guest of Cayden's Hall, having helped Saphira out of a difficult position a few years ago when fiends managed to infiltrate the basements beneath the temple—that area has since been intentionally collapsed. He uses the Hall as his base of operations in the Inner Sea, and is often sought out by Caydenites who need help dealing with undead menaces, due to his particular hatred of the unliving.

| SAPHIRA | CR 8 |
|---|---|

**XP 4,800**

Female human cleric of Cayden Cailean 9

CG Medium humanoid (human)

**Init** +1; **Senses** Perception +7

**DEFENSE**

**AC** 19, touch 13, flat-footed 17 (+5 armor, +1 deflection, +1 Dex, +1 dodge, +1 natural)

**hp** 62 (9d8+18)

**Fort** +7, **Ref** +4, **Will** +10

**OFFENSE**

**Speed** 30 ft.

**Melee** *+1 rapier* +8/+3 (1d6+1/18–20)

**Special Attacks** channel positive energy 5/day (DC 16, 5d6), might of the gods (+9, 9 rounds/day)

**Domain Spell-Like Abilities** (CL 9th; concentration +13)

At will—*dimensional hop* (90 feet/day)

7/day—*strength surge* (+4)

**Cleric Spells Prepared** (CL 9th; concentration +13)

5th—*righteous might, teleport*D

4th—*chaos hammer* (DC 18), *freedom of movement, neutralize poison, spell immunity*D

3rd—*dispel magic, fly*D, *invisibility purge, remove curse, remove disease*

2nd—*augury, bull's strength*D, *lesser restoration, make whole, remove paralysis, zone of truth*

1st—*ant haul*APG (DC 15), *bless water* (DC 15), *command* (DC 15), *detect evil, doom* (DC 15), *longstrider*D

0 (at will)—*create water, detect poison, mending, read magic*

**D** domain spell; **Domains** Strength, Travel

**STATISTICS**

**Str** 10, **Dex** 13, **Con** 12, **Int** 10, **Wis** 18, **Cha** 14

**Base Atk** +6; **CMB** +6; **CMD** 19

**Feats** Blind-Fight, Catch Off-Guard, Combat Casting, Dodge, Toughness, Weapon Focus (rapier)

**Skills** Appraise +6, Craft (alchemy) +6, Diplomacy +14, Heal +10, Knowledge (local) +3, Knowledge (religion) +12, Perception +7, Sense Motive +10

**Languages** Common

**SQ** agile feet (7/day)

**Combat Gear** alchemist's fire, holy water (2), tanglefoot bag, thunderstone; **Other Gear** *+1 chain shirt, +1 rapier, amulet of natural armor +1, ring of protection +1,* silver holy symbol of Cayden Cailean, 55 gp

## GAZETTEER

Through the centuries, several features have remained consistent through the incarnations of Cayden's Hall: a cask room, a garden, a main hall, an oratorium, the Shades, and the Walk of Thrones. Various heads of the loosely organized church have emphasized some elements over others as it suits them—one of the few privileges of rank that the haphazard church offers. In its newest layout, High Priestess Saphira's love of open-air gardens shows in the vastly expanded flora around the main hall, as well as in the presence of brightly colored lanterns.

### 1. FOUNTAIN (CR 1)

Cayden's Hall offers drinks to all of its patrons, as well as to its patrons' mounts and animal friends. Sparsely decorated with the tankard symbol of Cayden Cailean, the fountain favors function over form, with a basin two feet deep at the outer edge. Bowls, buckets, and cups of varying sizes are attached to iron chains along a wide sitting ledge, allowing for any to drink free of charge.

**Creature:** On more than one occasion, a long night of hard drinking has led an inebriated celebrant to the Hall's fountain to dunk his head (or his entire body) within the fountain's waters. During the nighttime hours, there is a 10% chance that there is such a person in the fountain, or lying next to it after being pulled out by either a companion or a Caydenite acolyte tasked with checking to make sure no one drowns. Festivals and city-wide celebrations increase this chance to 25%.

| TYPICAL CELEBRANT | CR 1 |
|---|---|

**XP 40**

Squire (*Pathfinder RPG NPC Codex* 251)

**hp** 19

### 2. WELL

In the past, this well provided all the water for Cayden's Hall, which was laboriously hauled up bucket by bucket. The Hall's latest rebuild includes a system that pipes water into the fountain, making it a much more convenient source of water for everybody with considerably less effort involved. The well is now

inner sea temples

Sacred Spaces and Profane Places

Cathedral of Exquisite Agony

Cayden's Hall

First Colonial Bank of Sargava

High Temple of Pharasma

House of Dawn's Redemption

Imvrildara

CAYDEN'S HALL

1 SQUARE = 5 FEET

disused, but some still toss coins into its maw hoping for a bit of the Accidental God's favor.

**Treasure:** A coin trap captures most coins tossed into the well. Once per month, the trap is emptied and the proceeds are donated to a local orphanage. A character who succeeds at a DC 30 Perception check locates the hidden mechanism that raises and lowers the trap, which usually contains 1d2 gp, 1d10 sp, and 1d100 cp.

## 3. Foyer

Rough-hewn stone blocks pave the entryway into the Hall proper, leading to a small foyer whose stretches curved ceiling 12 feet high. Mud-splattered cloaks, muck-encrusted boots, haversacks, packs, and walking sticks litter the area, hanging from hooks or shoved under benches. A sign hanging from one wall states, "You Leave It, You Loan It" in five different languages. Each dawn, when the Hall's staff closes its doors to clean and grab some sleep, anything left here is picked up and stashed behind a bar or in a storage room. A tally is kept of what's been left behind. Anyone who can give a reasonable description of an item collected here and roughly what night it was left can reclaim it. In the meanwhile, the Caydenite priests loan out the equipment to anyone who seems to need it to pursue a good cause that would meet with the Accidental God's approval. Sometimes down-on-their-luck or beginning adventurers get their first shield, torch, or weapon as a loaner from such leftover equipment. This gear is supposed to be returned within 90 days, but no one at the Hall worries about the equipment being returned late or damaged (though someone who fails to bring back borrowed gear must tell a very good story explaining why before being allowed to borrow any other equipment). Rarely, wealthy (or drunk) adventurers flush from a rich trove even opt to leave minor magic items here intentionally, in the hope of aiding a Caydenite in need.

**Treasure:** Roughly 200 gp worth of mundane adventuring gear is stored in the foyer at any one time, belonging to carousers in the main hall (area **9**).

## 4. Walk of Thrones (CR 2)

Three curved wooden bar counters with casks piled high behind them can be found in this room. Padded stools of varying age, the cushions ranging from brand new to well-worn, are set in front of them. Smooth flagstones, polished by the passage of feet, are broken up by a 20-foot-wide mosaic of a tankard.

**Creatures:** Normally three junior clergy attend the area as "bar wardens," who act as bartenders and also watch for anyone that might cause problems. Some bar wardens stay for a few weeks. Others remain for years and eventually gain positions of greater authority.

The stat block below can be used for any typical bar warden, and the following NPCs are offered as specific examples of bar wardens. Agyros, a native of Absalom and a beneficiary of the church's generosity as an orphan, has dedicated his life to Cayden Cailean and plans on serving at Cayden's Hall until the next Ascendance Day. Elematia often claims she has elven blood and got kicked out of Kyonin trying to prove it—and this is just one of the tall tales that she uses to keep the mood light and the customers happily buying ale. Lambys is unusually tall and doesn't say much, spending most of her time listening to her customers tell their woes.

| BAR WARDEN | CR 2 |
|---|---|

**XP 200**

Human cleric of Cayden Cailean 1

NG Medium humanoid (human)

**Init** +0; **Senses** Perception +2

---
**DEFENSE**

**AC** 11, touch 10, flat-footed 11 (+1 armor)

**hp** 12 (1d8+4)

**Fort** +3, **Ref** +0, **Will** +4

---
**OFFENSE**

**Speed** 30 ft.

**Melee** club +1 (1d6+1)

**Special Attacks** channel positive energy 5/day (DC 12, 1d6)

**Domain Spell-Like Abilities** (CL 1st; concentration +3)

5/day—*strength surge* (+1), *touch of chaos*

**Cleric Spells Prepared** (CL 1st; concentration +3)

1st—*bless*[D], *comprehend languages*, *divine favor*

0 (at will)—*create water*, *guidance*, *purify food and drink* (DC 12)

**D** domain spell; **Domains** Chaos, Strength (Resolve[APG] subdomain)

---
**STATISTICS**

**Str** 12, **Dex** 10, **Con** 13, **Int** 10, **Wis** 15, **Cha** 14

**Base Atk** +0; **CMB** +1; **CMD** 11

**Feats** Selective Channeling, Toughness

**Skills** Diplomacy +6, Heal +6, Knowledge (religion) +4

**Languages** Common

**Combat Gear** *scroll of remove fear*, *scroll of sanctuary*, alchemist's kindness[APG] (5), healer's kit; **Other Gear** padded armor, club, tankard, silver holy symbol of Cayden Cailean, 28 gp, 9 sp, 8 cp

## 5. The Shades (CR 1/2)

Decorated with woven rugs in vibrant hues of emerald, azure, and crimson and strewn with floor pillows in similar jewel tones, the Shades are a pair of private rooms on the southeastern side of Cayden's Hall. Woolen tapestries decorate the interior walls of the room, and thick curtains block the entries. Perfect for clandestine meetings where a modicum of privacy is required, these rooms can be reserved ahead of time for a modest fee (5 gp), which includes a round of refreshing beverages. True security is not guaranteed, but the Pathfinder

Inner Sea Temples

Sacred Spaces and Profane Places

Cathedral of Exquisite Agony

Cayden's Hall

First Colonial Bank of Sargava

High Temple of Pharasma

House of Dawn's Redemption

Imvrildara

Society has been satisfied with use of the Shades in its dealings.

**Creatures:** Unknown to the residents of Cayden's Hall, a clockwork spy was left behind by a member of the Aspis Consortium in the hope of overhearing the Pathfinder Society's plans.

| CLOCKWORK SPY | CR 1/2 |
|---|---|

**XP 200**

**hp** 5 (*Pathfinder RPG Bestiary 3* 58)

**Treasure:** A total of 10 gp, 25 sp, and 50 cp can be found among the cushions, throw pillows, and lap blankets, as well as a number of old broadsheets advertising various local businesses of interest to adventurers.

## 6. Patio

The scent of honeysuckle and jasmine permeates the tiled patio, along with the omnipresent hum of bees. This is a common area for Caydenites who are looking for someplace quieter to enjoy a drink and some company, tell tales, play a few classic board games, and take in the night air.

This is the normal nightly hangout of **Gillyfoile** (CG female halfling rogue 5; *Pathfinder RPG NPC Codex* 146), a member of the Bellflower Network. When nothing important seems to be going on, she sits contentedly and sips from a pot of tea as she plays checkers against herself. PCs seeking to aid (or join) the abolitionist organization can be directed to speak with this blonde-haired, brown-eyed halfling.

## 7. Gardens (CR 5)

An astonishing variety of plants grows on the southern side of the temple grounds, all of them associated with the production of alcoholic beverages in some manner. Apple and peach trees are the most prominent, but tall wooden posts with twining hops can also be found in the garden. Closer to the Main Hall (area 9), low hyssop plants hug the walls of the building.

**Creatures:** Most folk assume that Cayden's Hall employs a druid to take care of the gardens, and High Priestess Saphira continues to encourage this belief. In truth, a gang of brownies has taken up residence in the Hall's garden, and its services are paid for in fine whiskey, fresh-baked bread, and milk.

| BROWNIES (4) | CR 1 |
|---|---|

**XP 400 each**

**hp** 4 each (*Pathfinder RPG Bestiary 2* 49)

## 8. Confessional

Situated in the middle of the northeastern bar in the Walk of Thrones, the confessional is a simple affair, meant for private one-on-one conversations between one of the Hall's clergy and a supplicant, almost always over a drink.

**Treasure:** The plain wooden table in the confessional has clean stoles bearing the tankard symbol of Cayden Cailean, as well as bottles of absinthe[UE], applejack[UE], mead[UE], and oldlaw whiskey[UE] and two bottles of fine wine. In addition, the table functions as an altar of Cayden Cailean (*Pathfinder Campaign Setting: Inner Sea Gods* 246).

## 9. Main Hall

Heavy oak tables fill the main room of Cayden's Hall. Some are set low to the ground, but most are twice that height. Stacks of neatly cut firewood stand ready in corners to fuel the fire pit, and memorial tankards dedicated to the departed faithful sit atop the rafters that support the dome. From noon to dawn, the Main Hall welcomes customers representing all the citizens of Absalom, from all levels of society. The evening brings the biggest crowds, drawn in by the best entertainment, and raucous singing can be heard for blocks around Cayden's Hall. The bar in the southwestern corner of the room serves finger foods ready to eat, mostly in the form of hand pies, but also provides skewers of meat and vegetables that can be cooked on the grills (area 10).

## 10. Fire pit

Without fail, every previous version of Cayden's Hall has burned down—the mixing of alcohol and open flame was often a large factor. In an effort to delay the inevitable, High Priestess Saphira has installed a new stone-lined firepit. The pit has skewers of food cooking over it most of the time, and streamers that hang from the rafters well above the reach of the flames flutter in the rising smoke. The fire pit provides enough light to illuminate the hall and the Oratorium stage (area 11), mostly eliminating the need for candles or lanterns at individual tables.

Patrons wishing to prove a boast involving fire, or who are so drunk they seem likely to fall into the fire pit (or end up knocking something large or valuable and flammable into the pit) are generally moved out to the beer garden by acolytes or regular customers. Only the most trusted of allies are given much leeway in this regard, including a few trusted cooks and adventures, though Saphira also relaxes her rules if a friendly druid is nearby and able to cast *quench*. Sahira doesn't blame herself for being in charge when the last Cayden's Hall burned to the ground, but she also doesn't plan to repeat the experience.

## 11. Oratorium

An oval platform thirty feet long and 20 feet across, the Oratorium serves as a stage for musical performances from all cultures, from Qadiran poetry to epic sagas from the Lands of the Linnorm Kings. Covered lanterns provide additional illumination in a variety of colors. The Oratorium stage also serves as a location where dueling dares can be performed.

**Treasure:** A trap door in the center of the stage leads to a 3-foot-deep crawl space, which stores 1,000 gp of theater equipment in the form of costumes and backdrops. A masterwork fiddle made of bleached driftwood and silver and ivory fittings is wrapped in a particularly gaudy and tattered yellow robe.

## 12. MEZZANINE

Rising 15 feet above the Main Hall, the mezzanine is accessible only from the high priestess's quarters (area **13**) and gives a grand view of the Main Hall. The mezzanine also connects to the rafters, allowing retrieval and storage of any memorial mugs. Though it sits above her bedroom, High Priestess Saphira has been too busy to enjoy the privacy of the mezzanine much. Four Medium creatures can comfortably view the Oratorium stage (area **11**) from the chairs placed up here.

## 13. HIGH PRIESTESS'S QUARTERS

In her private quarters, High Priestess Saphira displays mementos of her Varisian upbringing and stores the materials needed to run Cayden's Hall. This small room holds stacks of papers, arranged in piles of controlled chaos, next to small casks, flasks, bottles, and wineskins. Knickknacks and keepsakes are displayed on shelves and set carefully at corners of the room. A ladder stretches toward the ceiling, its exit obscured by tapestries of constellations and butterflies.

Some might assume that Saphira's personal belongings were of great value to her, given their prominence. But she views the small bottles that litter her bedroom and the safety of her customers as far more valuable than even her familial kapenia; she chose to save her flock over the scarf during the temple's most recent fire.

**Treasure:** The samples of alcohol could fetch up to 200 gp when sold to the right buyer.

Among Saphira's personal belongings are a rock crystal wine carafe worth 100 gp, a silver and gold-filigreed samovar set worth 50 gp, and an assortment of jewelry in the Varisian style worth 500 gp in total.

## 14. CASK ROOM

Railings and tracks allow casks to be rolled up easily from cold storage—a room with the same dimensions that acts as a small subbasement of the cask room—and they are placed here before being moved out to the other bars (areas **4** and **15**). This area also serves as a communal sleeping chamber for any of the Hall's priests who don't have their own quarters and prefer not to sleep on the patio or in other rooms.

## 15. BEER GARDEN (CR 4)

During warm and temperate months, this part of Cayden's Hall allows enjoyment of the sunshine and open air. Hops and fruiting vines line the garden's sides, creating a living wall of green, while overhead, a crimson canvas awning blocks out the sun on the hottest days of summer. Glass tankards in multicolored hues hang above, burned candle stumps and spent lamp wicks in their bases. A large table supports three large beer kegs, while a locked box is set into a smaller table beside it.

High Priestess Saphira set up these self-serve beer kegs in part to encourage charitable donations toward Absalom's orphanages, but also to encourage competition and creativity for brewers. The three keg spaces are given to new brewers, or established brewers trying new recipes, with Cayden's Hall providing an excellent testing ground for their wares.

**Creature:** An ataxian has taken up residence in the beer garden, drawn in by the new beers on display here.

| ATAXIAN | CR 4 |
| --- | --- |

**XP 1,200**

**hp** 30 (*Pathfinder Campaign Setting: Inner Sea Gods* 283)

**Treasure:** The lockbox contains roughly 50 sp and 100 cp. On festival days, it often contains twice as much silver and copper, and up to an extra 100 gp.

SAPHIRA

INNER SEA TEMPLES

Sacred Spaces and Profane Places

Cathedral of Exquisite Agony

Cayden's Hall

First Colonial Bank of Sargava

High Temple of Pharasma

House of Dawn's Redemption

Imvrildara

## CAYDEN CAILEAN MAGIC

The following section details spells and magic items favored by priests of Cayden's Hall.

### CAYDEN CAILEAN MAGIC ITEMS

A number of different magical items have made their way to or from the church of Cayden Cailean, often taking the form of drinking vessels—a doubly useful gift, as his faithful might say.

| CENSURING PLACARD | | PRICE 14,300 GP |
|---|---|---|
| SLOT none | CL 10th | WEIGHT 2 lbs. |
| AURA moderate abjuration | | |

Most often appearing as a simple flattened board inscribed with a portion of Cayden Cailean's holy text, a *censuring placard* is used to inflict just punishment on offenders of church guidelines or to knock allies roughly back to their senses. A *censuring placard* functions as a *+1 club*. As a swift action with a successful melee attack, the wielder can use the placard to cast *break enchantment* on that target. Whether

this effort is successful or not, the *break enchantment* ability cannot be used again for a week.

| CONSTRUCTION REQUIREMENTS | COST 7,300 GP |
|---|---|
| Craft Magic Arms and Armor, *break enchantment* | |

| NEVERSPILL GOBLET | | PRICE 1000 GP |
|---|---|---|
| SLOT none | CL 3rd | WEIGHT 1 lb. |
| AURA faint conjuration | | |

The *neverspill goblet* was designed for one very simple purpose: to never have to worry about wasting Cayden Cailean's gifts. A goblet holds up to 1 cup of liquid (or 1 dose of a magic potable, such as a potion), and no matter how it is held or shaken, it never spills a drop, except down the throat of a willing drinker. A *neverspill goblet* does not dispense its contents for someone unwilling to drink from it. The magic of the goblet also keeps fluids from accidentally entering the goblet. This does not prevent poisoning (since the poisoner's addition is intentional), but means if a *neverspill goblet* is placed underwater and removed, its original contents remain undiluted. It is therefore possible to drink a potion from a *neverspill goblet* while underwater. Most *neverspill goblets* are made from light, portable materials such as wood or pewter, or come in larger sizes. Its magical nature does not prevent it from corrosion by acid. Liquids placed in a *neverspill goblet* do not succumb to the ravages of temperature or time, a fact that more than one adventurer has taken advantage of on journeys.

| CONSTRUCTION REQUIREMENTS | COST 500 GP |
|---|---|
| Craft Wondrous Item, *gentle repose* | |

| PARTING GLASS | | PRICE 23,000 GP |
|---|---|---|
| SLOT none | CL 12th | WEIGHT 1 lb. |
| AURA strong enchantment | | |

Not every adventurer returns to the tavern, and Cayden's Hall has seen many a drink raised in remembrance of a fallen comrade. A *parting glass*, engraved with the names of adventuring companies and their honored dead, is a rare gift given by senior priests of Cayden Cailean's church to survivors of quests that fit with the church's ideals but demanded a high cost.

Once per day when used in a toast with at least one other creature, a single creature drinking from a *parting glass* gains a +5 morale bonus on the next saving throw it attempts within 24 hours, and one poison (other than alcohol) currently affecting the drinker is targeted by *neutralize poison*.

| CONSTRUCTION REQUIREMENTS | COST 11,500 GP |
|---|---|
| Craft Wondrous Item, *greater heroism*, *neutralize poison* | |

| THUNDERING COLLAR | | PRICE 4,800 GP |
|---|---|---|
| SLOT neck | CL 1st | WEIGHT 1 lb. |
| AURA minor abjuration | | |

Made of twisted copper wire braided into a torc with red-stained dog paws at its ends, a *thundering collar* is so named after Cayden Cailean's faithful red mastiff, Thunder. A *thundering collar* allows the wearer to issue a rumbling growl that sounds like rolling thunder three times per day. Creatures within 15 feet must succeed at a DC 12 Will save to attack (as if affected by *sanctuary*). The wielder can bestow the effect on one adjacent ally as well. This effect lasts for 3 rounds or until the wearer or its ally attacks.

| CONSTRUCTION REQUIREMENTS | COST 2,400 GP |
| --- | --- |

Craft Wondrous Item, *ghost sound*, *sanctuary*

| WATCHFUL TANKARD | | PRICE 30,000 GP |
| --- | --- | --- |
| SLOT none | CL 5th | WEIGHT 10 lbs. |
| AURA faint divination | | |

Images of a dwarf and human drinking together decorate the sides of this 1-foot-tall granite stein, which is capped off with a rough-hewn orb of the same material. When the user speaks the command word and places a *watchful tankard* on a solid surface, such as a cavern ceiling or wooden table, the stein adheres to the surface (with the equivalent of an 18 Strength score). The last creature to drink from the stein can attempt Perception checks from the stein's location, as well as from its own, as long as it is within 60 feet of the *watchful tankard*. Any permanent vision-based bonuses (such as darkvision, low-light vision, or permanent *arcane sight*) are also usable through the *watchful tankard* but are limited to a range of 30 feet. It is possible to attempt Perception checks from the stein's point of view only while it is adhered to a solid surface in this way. Grabbing the handle and repeating the command word frees the *watchful tankard* from this location.

| CONSTRUCTION REQUIREMENTS | COST 15,000 GP |
| --- | --- |

Alertness, Craft Wondrous Item, *alarm*

## CAYDEN CAILEAN SPELLS

Some of Cayden Cailean's followers have created useful spells that are often taught and traded at Cayden's Hall.

### FERMENT

**School** transmutation; **Level** alchemist 1, bard 1, cleric 1, druid 1, sorcerer/wizard 1, witch 1
**Casting Time** 1 standard action
**Components** V, S, M (a drop of ale, mead, or wine)
**Range** touch
**Target** object touched
**Duration** 10 minutes/level
**Saving Throw** Fortitude negates (object); **Spell Resistance** yes (object)

This spell temporarily imbues a potable liquid (including elixirs, extracts, potions, and poisons) with an intoxicant. The caster must succeed at a caster level check in order to affect magic liquids and poisons (DC = 10 + item level for magic liquids, DC equal to the poison's save DC for a poison); otherwise, the spell fails. If the caster succeeds, the liquid also assumes a flavor according to what the caster desires,

but the effect on the imbiber is the same. An imbiber of a liquid affected by *ferment* must succeed at a Fortitude saving throw at the spell's save DC or take a –2 penalty on attack rolls, saves, ability checks, and skill checks for the remaining duration of the spell. Additionally, the DC of any skill check to identify a magic liquid or poison under the effects of this spell increases by 5.

### FREE SPIRIT

**School** abjuration; **Level** bard 3, cleric 3, druid 3, medium 3, shaman 3, spiritualist 3, witch 3
**Casting Time** 1 standard action
**Components** V, S
**Range** personal
**Target** you
**Duration** 1 minute/level

This spell allows you to channel the essence of Cayden Cailean's philosophy, giving you the benefits of a *freedom of movement* spell and granting you a +4 bonus on saving throws against fear effects. The spell also makes you drunk. For the duration of the spell, you take a –2 penalty on attack rolls, ability checks, skill checks, and concentration checks. If you somehow remove or avoid these penalties, the spell's duration ends.

### KNOCK, MASS

**School** transmutation; **Level** cleric 6, inquisitor 6, mesmerist 6, occultist 6, psychic 6, sorcerer/wizard 6
**Casting Time** 1 standard action
**Components** V
**Range** close (25 ft. + 5 ft./level)
**Target** one means of closure/level, no two of which can be more than 30 feet apart
**Duration** instantaneous
**Saving Throw** none; **Spell Resistance** no

Also known as "unshackle," this spell functions as *knock*, but works on multiple means of closure at once.

### SPIRIT SHARE

**School** transmutation; **Level** alchemist 1, bard 1, cleric 1, druid 1, occultist 1, shaman 1, sorcerer/wizard 1, witch 1
**Casting Time** 1 standard action
**Components** V, S, F (liquid to be shared)
**Range** personal
**Target** you
**Duration** 1 round/level

This spell was first created as a minor parlor trick, but adventuring Caydenites have repurposed and improved on it for use on their travels. For the duration of the spell, as a standard action you can touch a willing target to deliver 1 dose of a potable liquid (including alcoholic drinks and potions and elixirs, but not poisons or other liquids that are primarily harmful when drunk) in your possession (though not necessarily held in hand) into her.

inner sea temples

Sacred Spaces and Profane Places

Cathedral of Exquisite Agony

Cayden's Hall

First Colonial Bank of Sargava

High Temple of Pharasma

House of Dawn's Redemption

Imvrildara

# FIRST COLONIAL BANK OF SARGAVA

Sitting upon the highest peak within the city, the First Colonial Bank's gold-capped dome fuels Sargava's imagination with visions of the riches held within. Spoken of in reverent tones by merchants and Mwangi civilians but only seen by select clergy members, the temple's main vault is legendary for its security and treasures. I have heard rumors from my guide that a minority of Kalabuta view the temple as a remnant of Chelish occupation and bureaucracy, but those in the trade industry realize the temple's importance and promote the Wealthy Father as a deliverer who saved them from their lot as second-class citizens.

—From the writings of Kavas Tellen, devout priest of Abadar and Chelish banker

The First Colonial Bank of Sargava is the center of Abadaran worship in the southern Sargavan city of Kalabuto, and the city's primary center of commerce. Archbanker Batulu Senzan (see page 27) has presided over the temple since its construction and has worked tirelessly to grow his congregation. Introduced by Chelish colonials, the faith has remained despite the typical negative connotation of northern influences. This positive view of the church is due in part to the beliefs that worship of Abadar can pull one out of the depths of destitution, and that servitude keeps one in the good graces of wealth.

The archbanker has made the temple one of the more potent moderating forces in the city, ever eager to remind the governing body of its responsibilities to its citizens. Although the temple's acts might seem charitable, the church of Abadar is most concerned with the just enactment of laws and the continued flow of trade. The first floor accommodates the general public with its offices for securing loans and holding private meetings,

and the majority of its lobby is given over to the business of banking. The senior banker and archbanker hold sermons in the main chapel every Starday night. The floor below holds the vault and the quarters of a small number of resident priests needed for the daily services of cleaning, cooking, and security.

## HISTORY

The First Colonial Bank of Sargava is a relatively new construction in comparison with other nearby structures. The stone ziggurat upon which it is built was sacked by Mzali forces during their most recent incursion into Kalabuto in 4702 AR. After these forces destroyed the old monument that stood as a regal reminder of the past Kalabuta leader, the property was bought by the clergy of Abadar. This purchase was supported by the city's governor, General Alban, who felt the presence of the church of Abadar would draw in more foreign investors to the region and help secure the local economy. The temple was completed in 4708 AR and has been in service

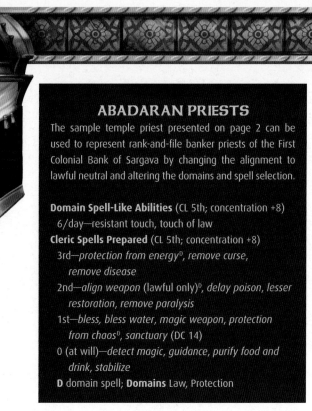

bankers have shown their dedication and accuracy with records in their clerkships and finally undergoing the trial of locks. Their instructor, Senior Banker Ninata Kala (see page 27), sets them in small study groups called branches. They delegate tasks to lower branches within the temple in a militaristic chain of command. The senior banker keeps these branches on task and answers only to Archbanker Senzan.

The clergy encourages the locals to trade with honesty and to hold to the letter of the law. The priests teach cooperation, equality, and the use of neighborly behavior to enhance one's individual wealth. The church never donates healing services, unless it is to those in service of the church, such as Kalabuto's military or political allies.

All the clergy of the temple have one final duty: upholding security. The largest financial losses the temple has ever faced have come through accepting counterfeit coins, false magic items, or even cursed items. Junior bankers pass the coins deposited by customers before the watchful eyes of Ninata to prevent any fake currency from hitting the till. The senior banker's duty is to ask clients withdrawing money to verify their identity to prevent fraudulent activity; this may, at times, involve scanning clients through magical means to ensure that no deception is possible. All clergy members undergo personal combat training and rigorous drills of mock robberies to prepare them for unexpected circumstances, and this fact is widely advertised within the city.

for the past eight years. As a militarized town, Kalabuto has come to see the temple as civilization's last hope at prosperity and seeks to protect it from destruction at the hands of invading forces.

## ORGANIZATION

The temple staff is composed of a mere 20 members in total, though the temple is capable of hiring scores of additional workers, guards, and scribes if the need arises. Most of the staff are new acolytes, just beginning their studies of the deity and still residing in off-temple lodgings. A select handful of clergy, referred to as junior bankers, actually live within the bank's walls. These junior

## MEMBERSHIP AND RELATIONS

Kalabuto's major population consists of nearly 10,000 Mwangi citizens. Most of the populace uses the First Colonial Bank of Sargava—the temple that shines like the sun in the morning light—as a landmark when giving directions within the city, but only a small percentage actually attends sermons. The parishioners are primarily colonists, but due to the archbanker's Mwangi heritage, a steady increase of local tribesfolk has begun. The word of Abadar has spread through the poor and those who have suffered at the hands of others; they come to alleviate their distress and see that local laws are upheld. All are welcome who venerate the Master of the First Vault, from lowly peddlers to investors, accountants, entrepreneurs, caravan guides, deal-makers, moneylenders, the wealthy owners of trading companies, and so on.

Those wishing to become members of the clergy must show dedication by tithing and purchasing a holy symbol from the temple. After this, they may begin a clerkship, learning scripture, bookkeeping, tax laws, and complex math skills. They must also set a good example to other citizens by maintaining the appearance of prosperity in manner and dress, even in periods of hardship. To become a junior banker, one must cultivate a strong mental attitude. A junior banker is a clergy member and banking adept who is able to give clients financial advice on matters relating to loans, investments, savings, and the teachings of Abadar. Their counsel not only helps clients to resolve financial issues, but also increases the temple's profits.

The temple has positive relations with many Mwangi Kalabuta, as Batulu is a charismatic man who shows a great deal of compassion for his fellow Mwangi citizens—even when upholding the bank-temple's profitable endeavors.

## NOTABLE DENIZENS

Without doubt, the most important member of the First Colonial Bank is Archbanker Senzan. His efforts to spread the worship of the Master of the First Vault among the local Mwangi has done much to improve relations. However, it also causes some Mwangi tribes who see all of Sargava as an unacceptable conquest of their lands to view him as a traitor, and his presence as a thin veneer of legitimacy concealing what is still an attack on their culture.

| BATULU SENZAN | CR 9 |
|---|---|

**XP 6,400**

Male human cleric of Abadar 9/ranger 1

LN Medium humanoid (human)

**Init** +1; **Senses** Perception +12

### DEFENSE

**AC** 20, touch 12, flat-footed 19 (+7 armor, +1 deflection, +1 Dex, +1 natural)

**hp** 89 (10 HD; 9d8+1d10+39)

**Fort** +10, **Ref** +6, **Will** +9

### OFFENSE

**Speed** 40 ft. (30 ft. in armor)

**Melee** mwk longsword +8/+3 (1d8/19–20)

**Ranged** +1 heavy crossbow +5 (1d10+1/19–20)

**Special Attacks** channel positive energy 3/day (DC 14, 5d6), favored enemy (evil outsiders +2)

**Domain Spell-Like Abilities** (CL 9th; concentration +12)

At will—dimensional hop (90 feet/day)

6/day—inspiring word (4 rounds)

**Cleric Spells Prepared** (CL 9th; concentration +12)

5th—greater command$^D$ (DC 18), dazing spiritual weapon (DC 14)

4th—discern lies$^D$ (DC 17), spiritual ally$^{APG}$, tongues

3rd—dispel magic, fly$^D$, remove blindness/deafness, remove disease, wind wall

2nd—locate object$^D$, lesser restoration, silence (DC 15), spiritual weapon, status, summon monster II

1st—comprehend languages, floating disk$^D$, protection from chaos, remove fear, sanctuary (DC 14), shield of faith

0 (at will)—detect magic, detect poison, mending, read magic

**D** domain spell; **Domains** Nobility, Travel (Trade subdomain$^{APG}$)

### STATISTICS

**Str** 11, **Dex** 12, **Con** 14, **Int** 13, **Wis** 16, **Cha** 10

**Base Atk** +7; **CMB** +7; **CMD** 19

**Feats** Alertness, Combat Casting, Dazing Spell$^{APG}$, Point-Blank Shot, Precise Shot, Toughness

**Skills** Appraise +13, Craft (stonemasonry) +3, Knowledge (engineering) +4, Knowledge (local) +4, Knowledge (nobility) +7, Knowledge (religion) +13, Perception +12, Sense Motive +5, Spellcraft +13, Stealth –1, Survival +7, Swim –2

**Languages** Common, Halfling

**SQ** track +1, wild empathy +1

**Combat Gear** oil of magic vestment +1, wand of cure light wounds; **Other Gear** +1 breastplate, +1 heavy crossbow with 10 bolts, mwk longsword, amulet of natural armor +1, ring of protection +1, backpack, bedroll, belt pouch, candles (10), flint and steel, hemp rope (50 ft.), holy text (The Manual of City Building), silver holy symbol of Abadar, soap, spell component pouch, torches (10), trail rations (5), waterskin, 50 pp, 22 gp

His protegee, Senior Banker **Ninata Kala** (LG female human cleric of Abadar 8/expert 2), is the daughter of a prominent Chelish colonist and a high-ranking Mwangi tribeswoman. This allows Ninata a fair degree of clout within the cross-cultural population of Kalabuto. The senior banker deals with the more mundane aspects of the temple and is in charge of the day-to-day operations. In general, her responsibilities include addressing customers, processing special instructions on accounts,

inner sea temples

Sacred Spaces and Profane Places

Cathedral of Exquisite Agony

Cayden's Hall

First Colonial Bank of Sargava

High Temple of Pharasma

House of Dawn's Redemption

Imvrildara

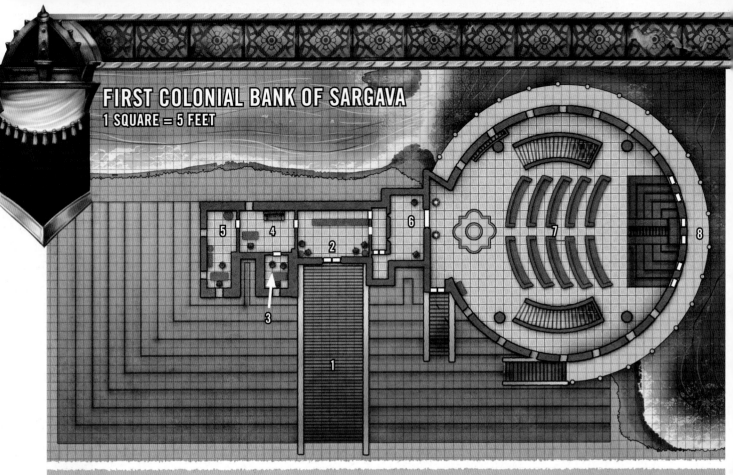

# FIRST COLONIAL BANK OF SARGAVA
1 SQUARE = 5 FEET

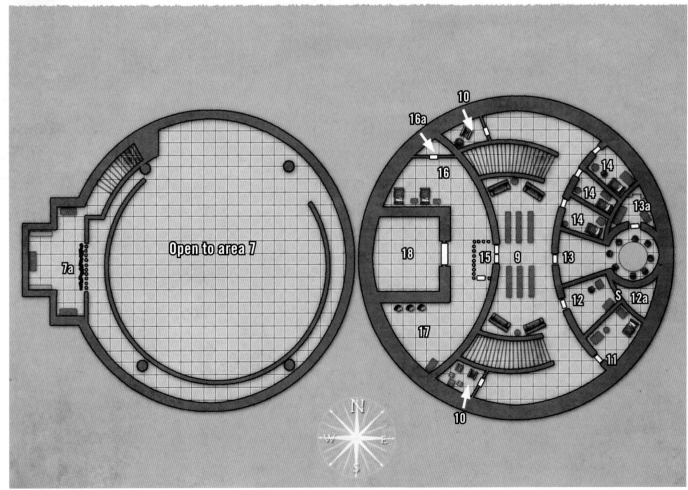

Open to area 7

and conducting general file maintenance. She performs daily office responsibilities such as composing customer correspondence, bookkeeping, cleaning and maintenance of holy items, ordering and preparing shipments, and collecting taxes. She also compiles and reviews the daily reports of the junior bankers. Most importantly, though, she is directly in charge of providing access to the main vault. Ninata also leads the education of the junior bankers in the teachings of Abadar and the temple rituals. She encourages her subordinates to serve as proactive members of their respective branches by taking lead roles and initiating sales for new and existing clients.

## GAZETTEER

Before the temple was constructed, the stones of the small ziggurat formed the base of a monument dedicated to Kalabuto's founding ruler. The clerics have long since removed all traces of that ancient leader from the temple grounds, and the reworked stone now supports the holy bank. As a carefully planned construction, the First Colonial Bank of Sargava has many standard features.

**Doors:** The temple's doors are some of the best crafted in all of Kalabuto. The outside doors are made from solid stone blocks (hardness 8, hp 30, break DC 25, Disable Device DC 25), while the security doors inside the temple are made of iron (hardness 10, hp 60, break DC 28, Disable Device DC 35), and they automatically lock when closed. Their locks are magical and require unconventional means to open—the touch of a holy symbol of Abadar, when wielded by a loyal worshiper of Abadar, unlocks a door for 1 minute. A successful *dispel magic* spell (DC 21 dispel check) unlocks one of these doors for 1d4 rounds.

**Walls:** The magically treated reinforced masonry walls (hardness 16, hp 540, break DC 70) have been infused with potent wards that render them resistant to teleportation and transmutation effects (such as *passwall*, *teleport*, or *transmute rock to mud*); in order to successfully affect or bypass one of the temple walls, the spellcaster must succeed at a DC 30 caster level check.

## 1. STAIRS

This set of steep stairs leads to the lobby. Printed public notices, including the temple's hours of operation, are posted on a wooden board next to the door.

## 2. TEMPLE LOBBY (CR 7)

The stone double door providing access to the temple is unlocked during business hours.

**Creatures:** Two clerks sit behind the large wooden counter to greet new patrons as they enter. **Varina** (LG female human cleric of Abadar 5) and **Callote** (LN male elf cleric of Abadar 5) work the counter with ink-stained fingers. Use the statistics for the standard Abadaran

priest (see the sidebar on page 26) for both these NPCs. Each of the doors is protected by a *greater glyph of warding*, designed to teleport any creature that is not a worshiper of Abadar to one of the jail cells of Kalabuto's constable.

## 3. SENIOR BANKER'S OFFICE (CR 5)

This simple office is crammed with tall bookcases and scroll racks.

**Creature:** Senior Banker Ninata Kala, an expert in tax law and tax collection, can normally be found here.

## 4. SCRIPTORIUM

This common room is used by acolytes and clerks to write contracts and discuss banking options with citizens. The parchments here contain details of various locals' financial accounts. Extensive study (5 hours or more) of these notes grants the researcher a +4 bonus on Knowledge (local) checks to gather information on citizens.

## 5. ARCHBANKER'S OFFICE

This office currently serves Archbanker Batulu Senzan as a private retreat and workshop. Mwangi paraphernalia adorns the office, including his old short spears and used set of hide armor. Batulu uses the northeastern table as a personal shrine for worship of Abadar.

**Treasure:** The holy symbol and various trinkets gathered here are worth 2,500 gp in all. The table covered with parchments and notes mostly contains detailed records of loans and laws that the archbanker is working on. The safe here is locked (Disable Device DC 35) and contains a portion of the archbanker's personal stash of gold coins worth 2,000 gp, an *iron golem manual*, and a *key cloak* (see page 32).

## 6. SECURITY CHECK (CR 7)

This antechamber is a security checkpoint. Visitors who enter through the lobby must first pass by the arrow slits and are greeted at the iron security door by a guard. The massive vault door that leads into the nave is meant more for show than as a real protective measure. Its only locking mechanism is a simple lock (Disable Device DC 20); one of the guards in the room normally carries the key.

**Creatures:** Two guards, Makmeth and Zoreg, manage this checkpoint. Zoreg is very personable and interviews those who wish to enter via the lobby through the iron security door while Makmeth trains her crossbow on them through an arrow slit. When traffic is light, the two sit in the comfortable leather chairs here and chat.

| MAKMETH AND ZOREG | CR 5 |
|---|---|

**XP 1,600 each**
LN female dwarf and LG male human
Expert bodyguard (*Pathfinder RPG NPC Codex* 269)
**hp** 59 each

inner sea temples

Sacred Spaces and Profane Places

Cathedral of Exquisite Agony

Cayden's Hall

First Colonial Bank of Sargava

High Temple of Pharasma

House of Dawn's Redemption

Imvrildara

## 7. Temple Nave (CR 2)

This immense chamber is where the weekly sermons are held. Its large, cathedral-like ceiling hosts the pride and joy of the temple: an incredible mural depicting Abadar clothed in a brilliant golden breastplate and silk robes. A large fountain sprays water high into the air to gently mist upon a large gold key, held aloft by a permanent *levitation* spell. Six doors that exit out onto the balcony (area **8**) stand behind the altar. Two sets of sweeping stone stairways with wooden railings descend to the floor below (area **9**). A smaller set of stairs leads up to the sacristy (area **7a**). An exterior door to the south allows direct access to the nave. On Starday nights, the clergy opens this door and greets worshipers, while the guards monitor from behind the partially open vault door that leads to area **6**.

**Creature:** Vorlai Sana is typically found deep in worship within the nave. Vorlai is a rare paladin of Abadar, drawn to the difficulties of Sargava in the hopes of finding a way to protect and expand civilization through just methods without allowing the rights of those threatened by an expanding Sargava to get trampled. She struggles to find a way to serve both her strong sense of righteousness and her duty to her god.

| VORLAI SANA | CR 2 |
|---|---|

**XP 600**

Haughty avenger (*Pathfinder RPG NPC Codex* 113)

**hp** 21

## 7a. Sacristy

Priests prepare for rituals on the upper balcony that overlooks the nave. Mirrors allow them to ensure their attire is in order. The cabinets contain incense, robes, and other mundane items necessary for conducting services.

**Treasure:** A successful DC 20 Perception check reveals a stash of 2 doses of *incense of meditation*.

## 8. Balcony

This deck wraps around the circular edge of the temple and gives a grand view of the waterfall and city below. A sturdy bannister prevents accidental falls due to the slippery floors (which imposes a –4 penalty on Acrobatic checks here) caused by the mists of the waterfall wafting over. The sounds of birdcalls and the gentle babble of the waterfall mingle here and attract any who wish peaceful solitude.

## 9. Temple Library

Several bookshelves contain an extensive collection of volumes, mainly on the subject of Abadar's church. Access to these resources along with 1d4 hours of study provides a +8 circumstance bonus on Knowledge checks pertaining to banking or Abadar.

## 10. Storage

The priests store dry food, wine, vestments, sacramental tools, extra candles, and other religious paraphernalia in these chambers. A small amount of cleaning supplies, a few stone-carving tools, and some writing materials are kept here for the scribes and custodian.

## 11. Senior Banker's Chambers

This room has been Ninata Kala's home for many years. This finely appointed room serves as a study, shrine, and bedchamber. The walls are decorated with staggeringly detailed maps of Kalabuto.

## 12. Archbanker's Chambers

This plush bedchamber holds a four-poster bed surrounded by oak furniture.

**Treasure:** The wardrobe is crammed with fine men's clothing—five noble's outfits, five priest's vestments, and one royal outfit. One of the dressing table drawers contains a jewelry box holding a silver chain worth 50 gp and a gold snuff box set with a topaz valued at 400 gp.

## 12a. Secret Vault

This chamber is hidden behind a locked secret panel (Perception DC 30, Disable Device DC 35), and only the archbanker carries the key or knows of its existence.

**Treasure:** This secret chamber holds a small amount of treasure that the archbanker is keeping in trust (to be used only to further the needs of the First Colonial Bank of Sargava) as well as important documents about local loans and agreements made by the church. The chest and safe in this room both bear a *greater glyph of warding*. The iron chest in the corner is locked (Disable Device DC 30). Inside are 35 gems worth 1,000 gp each. The safe contains a *potion of haste*, a *vaultbow* (see page 33), and a pair of *bracers of armor +4* emblazoned with holy symbols of Abadar.

## 13. Refectory

The immense table in this keyhole-shaped room bears a carved depiction of Abadar's First Vault. The temple priests take their meals and have meetings in this room.

## 13a. Kitchen

A large fireplace takes up most of this kitchen.

## 14. Priests' Cells

Each of these rooms is similarly furnished with a wooden bed, a cabinet, and a table with a chair.

## 15. Security Cage

Through the security door stands a barred iron cage. The guards must have direct permission from the archbanker to let anyone other than the senior banker or custodian inside. Weapon racks filled with polearms line one of the walls here.

## 16. Guards' Dormitory

Two cots, trunks, and a washstand fill this area where the off-duty guards usually sleep. They have been known to complain of occasional scratching sounds emanating from the privy (area **16a**).

## 16a. Privy (CR 5)

The privy is clean and unremarkable. A PC who succeeds at a DC 20 Perception check notices scratches in and around the toilet, as if something the size of a baby with claws had crawled through the hole many times. No one is sure what caused these markings. Several minor magical effects in this room keep the air fresh and the toilet clean. When the privy was originally built, it connected to what were believed to be trash pits in the original ziggurat structure on the foundation of which the First Colonial Bank of Sargava is built.

**Creature:** In truth, those original shafts connected to the hunting grounds of an ancient rat king that occasionally crawls up into the new construction but that has yet to venture any farther from the privy, though it is considering doing so.

| RAT KING | CR 5 |
|---|---|

**XP 1,600**

**hp** 57 (*Pathfinder RPG Bestiary 4* 225)

## 17. Training Area (CR 5)

Training dummies and other similar equipment mark this area as a combat training area. The custodian, Belios Valler, can be found here when he is not cleaning or fixing various things within the temple.

| BELIOS VALLER | CR 5 |
|---|---|

**XP 1,600**

Nimble shuriken thrower (*Pathfinder RPG NPC Codex* 98)

**hp** 40

## 18. Temple Vault (CR 13)

This room's only light source is a key-shaped lantern that hangs from a gold chain in the center of the vault. The door to the vault is trapped with a *greater glyph of warding*.

**Creature:** An iron golem stands outside this room. If anyone but the archbanker or the senior banker attempts to open the vault door, the guardian springs to life and moves at once to attack. Its orders prevent it from exiting this area, though it will pursue targets into the security cage. It obeys the archbanker, if he is present, or anyone that speaks a secret command word known only to the archbanker.

| IRON GOLEM | CR 13 |
|---|---|

**XP 25,600**

**hp** 129 (*Pathfinder RPG Bestiary* 162)

**Treasure:** The various stacks, chests, and coffers hold a total of 415,220 cp, 200,540 sp, 155,200 gp, 1,200 pp, and various art objects and items of jewelry worth 31,100 gp. Additionally, the vault contains a *rod of wonder* and a *ring of elemental command* (earth).

**Development:** The vault door (hardness 10, hp 100, break DC 35) is locked with an animated lock that actively works against attempts to be picked. Opening it requires three successful Disable Device checks in 3 consecutive rounds. The first of these checks has a DC of 30, the second a DC of 32, and the third a DC of 34.

BATULU SENZAN

inner sea temples

Sacred Spaces and Profane Places

Cathedral of Exquisite Agony

Cayden's Hall

First Colonial Bank of Sargava

High Temple of Pharasma

House of Dawn's Redemption

Imvrildara

## ABADARAN MAGIC

This section details magic options used by priests of the First Colonial Bank of Sargava.

### ABADARAN MAGIC ITEMS

The following magic items are favored by (and occasionally sold by) priests of the First Colonial Bank of Sargava.

| KEY CLOAK | | PRICE 20,000 GP |
|---|---|---|
| SLOT shoulders | CL 9th | WEIGHT 2 lbs. |
| AURA moderate conjuration | | |

This short cloak is made of gold thread spun into a pattern of interlocking key shapes. The cloak grants the wearer a +1 shield bonus to AC. As a move action, the wearer can activate the cloak, which instantly produces enough keys to wrap the wearer in a dome-shaped shield of hardened metal, protecting the wearer as if he were carrying a tower shield with which he is proficient. While using this ability, the wearer can take no other actions (other than adjusting which direction the effective tower shield is considered to be facing) and is immobile. The wearer can remain in this form indefinitely, but resting in this form is equivalent to resting in heavy armor. The dome of keys can be dismissed as a swift action, and it automatically vanishes if the cloak is removed.

Once per day, the cloak can also create a single special skeleton key as a standard action. This skeleton key can be tried on any one lock that uses a key, even if you aren't trained in the Disable Device skill. You use the key's Disable Device bonus of +15 rather than your own; you cannot take 10 when using a skeleton key. You can only attempt to open a particular lock with the skeleton key once. If the roll fails, the key is unable to open or close that lock. The key lasts for 1 hour and can be used on only a single lock during that time.

| CONSTRUCTION REQUIREMENTS | COST 10,000 GP |
|---|---|

Craft Wondrous Item, *fabricate, knock, stoneskin*

| MELTDOWN SAFE | | PRICE 10,000 GP |
|---|---|---|
| SLOT none | CL 3rd | WEIGHT 10 lbs. |
| AURA strong conjuration | | |

This iron safe is only 6 inches wide by 6 inches tall, but it opens into an extrtadimensional space—its inside is larger than its outside dimensions, as a type 1 *bag of holding*. The intricate lock on the door is of superior quality (Disable Device DC 40) and has a powerful security feature: if any attempt to pick the lock is unsuccessful, the inner space floods with magic fire and the contents begin taking 5d6 points of fire damage per round. After 10 rounds of extreme heat, the safe fully consumes itself and is reduced to a pile of ash. If the door is opened through any means during these 10 rounds, blasts of searing hot fire spew forth in a 15-foot cone that deals 5d6 points of fire damage (Reflex DC 23 half) for the remaining rounds.

| CONSTRUCTION REQUIREMENTS | COST 5,000 GP |
|---|---|

Craft Wondrous Item, *fire trap, secret chest*

| SECURE PAYPACK | | PRICE 4,000 GP |
|---|---|---|
| SLOT none | CL 9th | WEIGHT 5 lbs. |
| AURA moderate conjuration | | |

This rugged backpack is identical to a *handy haversack* in most regards, with numerous compartments for storing items. Any effort to identify it with a Spellcraft check result ranging from 24 to 33 by someone unfamiliar with its special properties reveals it to be a *handy haversack*. A result below 24 does not identify any magic properties, while a result of 34 or higher reveals its additional secret properties. It has two hidden compartments (Perception DC 35), each able to store up to 1 cubic foot of material or 10 pounds in weight. In addition, the entire item is reinforced with thin mithral fibers, giving it a hardness of 15 and 5 hit points. Each compartment has a concealed superior lock (Perception DC 35, Disable Device DC 40) built in to prevent unauthorized access. When a compartment is locked, an item can still be removed from it as a move action by a character who has a key to the lock, like a normal *handy haversack*. The keys are not magical and can be crafted (Craft DC 25) by a character able to disable the existing locks and who has at least 5 ranks in Craft (locks). Each *secure paypack* is normally created with two keys.

| CONSTRUCTION REQUIREMENTS | COST 2,000 GP |
|---|---|

Craft Wondrous Item, *arcane lock, knock, secret chest*

| UNIVERSAL LOCK | | PRICE 5,150 GP |
|---|---|---|
| SLOT none | CL 5th | WEIGHT 1/2 lb. |
| AURA faint abjuration | | |

This intricate padlock (hardness 10, hp 10, break DC 28, Disable Device DC 35) is crafted from pure gold and etched with depictions of the First Vault along its face. The lock can be placed onto any object that can open and close (such as a chest, pouch, door, window, or even a folded napkin, as well as magic items such as *bags of holding* and *portable holes*). The lock cannot be placed on a creature. Upon command, the lock merges with the item, becoming an inked image of the lock that covers half of the item being locked. If the item's hardness and normal hit points are lower than those of the *universal lock*, the item's hardness and hit points are increased to match those of the lock.

The *universal lock* remains in place until the owner commands it to unlock or it is successfully picked; it then reverts back to its original form. If the object it is locking is broken open, the *universal lock* is destroyed. A *knock* spell does not open an object sealed with a *universal lock*, but it reduces the lock's Disable Device DC by 5 for 10 minutes.

| CONSTRUCTION REQUIREMENTS | COST 2,650 GP |
|---|---|

Craft Wondrous Item, *arcane lock*, *hold portal*

## ABADARAN MAGIC WEAPONS

The following magic weapons are considered signs of significant wealth among bankers of the First Colonial Bank of Sargava.

| MACE OF KEYS | | PRICE 50,312 GP |
|---|---|---|
| SLOT none | CL 9th | WEIGHT 8 lbs. |
| AURA moderate transmutation | | |

The flanges on the head of this *+1 axiomatic heavy mace* are shaped like skeleton keys. Three times per day as a swift or immediate action when making a melee attack with the mace, the wielder can trigger this mace's unlocking ability. This ability must be declared before the melee attack is rolled, and if the attack is unsuccessful, the unlocking ability is wasted. Upon a successful melee attack with the mace while using the unlocking ability, the wielder can attempt a combat maneuver check against the target's CMD. On a success, the mace causes an item on the target in the belt, shoulder, or neck slot to come loose and fall to the ground in the target's space.

In addition, when attempting to destroy a lock, the mace ignores up to 20 points of the lock's hardness.

| CONSTRUCTION REQUIREMENTS | COST 25,312 GP |
|---|---|

Craft Arms and Armor, *knock*, *passwall*

| VAULTBOW | | PRICE 28,550 GP |
|---|---|---|
| SLOT none | CL 13th | WEIGHT 4 lbs. |
| AURA strong conjuration | | |

This *+1 light repeating crossbow* of deep mahogany rimmed with gold has a stock carved in the likeness of Abadar's First Vault. An extradimensional space within the crossbow can hold 20 bolts. Loading new bolts into the extradimensional space requires a move action that provokes an attack of opportunity for each bolt. The crossbow weighs the same no matter how many bolts are placed inside it. A worshiper of Abadar treats the *vaultbow* as a light crossbow for purposes of proficiency and applying the benefits of feats relating to a light crossbow.

Three times per day, the wielder can choose to have a bolt transform into a length of chain that wraps around its target on a successful attack. This decision must be made before the attack roll is made. A Large or smaller creature struck by this attack becomes entangled (and if dependent on wings to fly, it must succeed at a DC 15 Reflex save or lose the ability to fly while entangled). An entangled creature can break (and destroy) the chains with a successful DC 30 Strength check or escape them with a successful DC 30 combat maneuver check or Escape Artist check. This chain lasts for 5 rounds before fading from existence.

| CONSTRUCTION REQUIREMENTS | COST 14,550 GP |
|---|---|

Craft Arms and Armor, *chain of perdition*[UM], *secret chest*

## ABADARAN SPELLS

These spells are most commonly found in use by priests of the First Colonial Bank of Sargava.

### SOUL VAULT

**School** abjuration; **Level** cleric 3, druid 4, inquisitor 3, psychic 5, shaman 3, sorcerer/wizard 4, spiritualist 2, witch 4

**Casting Time** 1 standard action

**Components** V, S, DF

**Range** touch

**Target** creature touched

**Duration** 10 minutes/level

**Saving Throw** Will negates (harmless); **Spell Resistance** yes

This spell protects the target's soul by briefly enveloping the target in an ethereal vault. The target gains a +4 bonus on saving throws against spells and effects that would trap or redirect its soul (such as *magic jar*, *soul bind*, and *trap the soul*) and effects that would transform the target into an undead creature. The target is granted a save to negate such effects even if one is not normally allowed. If it's cast on a living creature that then dies, the target's body and spirit are protected by the spell for its duration. If it's cast on a corpse within 1 round of death, the target's body and soul are both protected. Otherwise, only the body receives the protection.

Any spellcaster that worships Abadar may learn and cast *soul vault* as a 4th level spell, if it isn't normally on her class spell list. *Soul vault* can be made permanent with the *permanency* spell at a cost of 7,500 gp and a minimum caster level of 11th.

### TRUE APPRAISAL

**School** divination; **Level** bard 1, cleric 1, inquisitor 1, occultist 1, witch 1

**Casting Time** 1 standard action

**Components** V, F (gold coin)

**Range** personal

**Target** you

**Duration** 8 hours

**Saving Throw** none; **Spell Resistance** no

You gain temporary insight into the value of objects. You gain a +5 competence bonus on Appraise checks, can attempt an Appraise check to determine an object's value as a move action, and can take 10 on an Appraise check even if stress or distractions would normally prevent you from doing so. You know if you fail an Appraise check, and you never determine a wildly inaccurate price.

inner sea temples

Sacred Spaces and Profane Places

Cathedral of Exquisite Agony

Cayden's Hall

First Colonial Bank of Sargava

High Temple of Pharasma

House of Dawn's Redemption

Imvrildara

# HIGH TEMPLE OF PHARASMA

"Imagine a tower so tall it pierces the sky." That is what they told me about the High Temple's Bone Spire, and naturally, it was an exaggeration, but not outrageously so.

Walking through the Necropolis of the Faithful was like traveling through time. I saw the pompous Sarenite tombs built during the Keleshite Interregnum, tombstones emblazoned with black sphinxes from the Second Age, and just outside the temple gates, hieroglyph-covered monuments from the First Age of Osirion.

I passed through the gates and gazed up at the magnificent spire. Before me opened an exquisite, fragrant garden. In a place so somber, I did not expect to see such beauty.

—From the memoirs of Ammuhab, Pharasmin pilgrim

Inner Sea
Temples

Sacred Spaces
and
Profane Places

Cathedral of
Exquisite Agony

Cayden's Hall

First Colonial
Bank of Sargava

High Temple
of Pharasma

House of Dawn's
Redemption

Imvrildara

Situated in the Sphinxside district of Sothis, the capital city of Osirion, the High Temple of Pharasma presides over the grounds of the Necropolis of the Faithful on the western bank of the Crimson Canal. In contrast to the gothic cathedrals of Pharasma typical in Avistani cities, the High Temple is built in a more traditional Osirian style. Large limestone blocks, painted in alternating horizontal stripes of blue and white, form the walls of the temple, which features a flat roof, narrow, arched windows, and a central courtyard open to the sky.

The temple's towering obelisk is one of the most prominent landmarks in Sothis. Built in the image of the impossibly tall spire atop which Pharasma's Boneyard sits, the 320-foot-tall Bone Spire is the second-highest structure in Sothis—only the Black Dome, the carapace of the great beetle Ulunat, is taller. The spire is constructed of massive, white granite blocks and treated with magic that makes the structure stronger than any edifice of natural stone.

## HISTORY

In the first centuries of the Age of Destiny, followers of many faiths began to flock to Sothis, the capital of the fledgling nation of Osirion, where they built temples to Abadar, Nethys, and Pharasma, among others. One of these early churches was the Shrine of the Graves, a simple prayer room on the west bank of the Crimson Canal, where priests performed funerary rites for the deceased and prepared bodies for burial. The church of Pharasma was very accepting of burying people of all creeds and backgrounds—in death, all are equal, as the Pharasmin saying goes.

Over the centuries, the Shrine of the Graves grew in wealth and power, and many new buildings were built near the old prayer room. By 1491 AR, when construction of the Bone Spire was completed, the Shrine of the Graves had far surpassed Osirion's other Pharasmin temples in size and significance, and it became known as the High Temple of Pharasma. Consequently, the temple's

rulers were just as dependent on the Pharasmin temple to bury their dead as the pharaohs before them had been.

When Khemet I was crowned pharaoh in 4609 AR and restored native Osirian rule to the country, a surge of nationalism swept the country, and many new monuments were built to honor Osirion's past. When the church of Nethys started rebuilding Azghaad's Spire, the High Temple of Pharasma donated a sizable sum of money for the construction project, under one very important condition: the new tower could not exceed the Bone Spire in height.

three high priests were considered the foremost seats of authority in the church hierarchy at that time.

In 1532 AR, Osirion became a satrapy controlled by the Padishah Empire of Kelesh, and the Keleshite invaders destroyed numerous monuments from Osirion's past, including Azghaad's Spire and many other cultural and religious landmarks. The Bone Spire suffered no such desecration, however, perhaps because the Keleshite

## ORGANIZATION

Most priests at the High Temple of Pharasma are clerics or oracles, and more than half of them are women. The priests' main duties include maintaining the graves and tombs of the Necropolis of the Faithful, performing funerary rituals, comforting those who have lost loved ones, and overseeing births. All priests wear black robes and carry a ceremonial dagger called a skane.

At the top of the hierarchy is a council of three high priests who represent the three aspects of the Pharasmin faith: birth, death, and fate. Although the three are technically equals, the high priest of death usually has more responsibilities and influence than the other two because the temple's main function is to take care of the Necropolis of the Faithful. The high priests each bear a symbol related to the aspect of the faith they represent on the right sleeve of their black robes.

Outside the church's formal hierarchy exists another Pharasmin organization, the Order of the Nightjar. The Nightjars are grim, dutiful slayers of the undead who emerge from their lodge after dark when the gates of the necropolis are locked and no visitors are present. They patrol the massive graveyard, destroying any haunts, wandering undead, or undead lairs that they find. Despite the protective funerary rites that the Pharasmin priests perform, a vast amount of necromantic energy accumulates in the necropolis, and undead activity is far from uncommon there. This is a closely guarded secret, as the church fears that the truth would harm its reputation and business. As the necropolis keeps growing, the secretive Nightjars—who don't even officially exist—have to spread their resources thin to cover more ground on their nightly missions.

Though all servants of Pharasma despise the undead as abominations, few are as dedicated and specialized in destroying the undead as the Nightjars. Most of the Nightjars are clerics, inquisitors, rangers, or warpriests, but diviners, hallowed necromancers, and occultists are also common. Because of the inherent dangers of the job and the rigorous training involved, everyone who joins the order is usually at least 4th level. The Nightjars use a secret whistled language called Nightsong that members can use to communicate with each other up to 500 feet away. Members of the order can learn this language by putting a rank in the Linguistics skill, but they are forbidden to teach the language to nonmembers. Nightjars wear cloaks of dark purple with a dagger-and-bird emblem embroidered in silver.

## MEMBERSHIP AND RELATIONS

There is a saying in Sothis that everyone will see the Bone Spire up close at least once—before they are buried in the Necropolis of the Faithful. The saying is not far from the truth; regardless of which faith they followed in life, most Sothans are indeed buried in the necropolis. As such, most people who visit the High Temple are mourners from various religious backgrounds. Nevertheless, Pharasma is one the most popular deities in Sothis and has a strong following that mainly consists of midwives, morticians, expectant mothers, fortune-tellers, and people whose lives were tragically changed by the loss of a loved one.

The largest and most prestigious of all Pharasmin temples in Garund, the High Temple occasionally sends priests to help and supervise other Pharasmin temples in Osirion and other parts of the continent, or to spread the faith into new regions. The High Temple is on mostly amicable terms with the temples of Abadar and Nethys (though there is some rivalry between the three faiths), and there is mutual respect between Ruby Prince Khemet III—Osirion's current ruler and a cleric of Abadar—and the three high priests of Pharasma's temple.

## NOTABLE DENIZENS

A prominent inhabitant of the High Temple of Pharasma is the ahmuuth psychopomp Ta-Hepu.

| TA-HEPU | CR 9 |
|---|---|

**XP 6,400**

Female ahmuuth psychopomp inquisitor of Pharasma 7 (*Pathfinder Campaign Setting: Inner Sea Gods* 303, *Pathfinder RPG Advanced Player's Guide* 38)

N Medium outsider (extraplanar, psychopomp)

**Init** +7; **Senses** darkvision 60 ft., low-light vision, spiritsense; Perception +20

### DEFENSE

**AC** 24, touch 13, flat-footed 21 (+4 armor, +3 Dex, +3 natural, +4 shield)

**hp** 110 (13 HD; 7d8+6d10+46)

**Fort** +15, **Ref** +9, **Will** +16

**Defensive Abilities** animated shield; **DR** 5/adamantine; **Immune** death effects, disease, poison; **Resist** cold 10, electricity 10; **SR** 15

### OFFENSE

**Speed** 30 ft.

**Melee** *+1 undead-bane returning dagger* +14/+9/+4 (1d4+3/19–20 plus 2d6 vs. undead), *+1 undead-bane returning dagger* +14/+9 (1d4+2/19–20 plus 2d6 vs. undead)

**Ranged** *+1 undead-bane returning dagger* +16 (1d4+3/19–20 plus 2d6 vs. undead)

**Special Attacks** bane (7 rounds/day), judgment 3/day, spirit touch

**Spell-Like Abilities** (CL 6th; concentration +6)

At will—*bleed* (DC 10), *deathwatch*, *detect undead*, *disrupt undead*, *ghost sound* (DC 10), *summon* (level 1, 1 great horned owl*[B3]* 100%)

3/day—*chill touch* (DC 11), *ghostbane dirge*[APG] (DC 12), *greater teleport* (self plus 50 lbs. of objects only), *silence* (DC 12), *spectral hand*

1/day—*ghostly disguise*[UM], *locate creature*, *speak with dead* (DC 13)

**Domain Spell-Like Abilities** (CL 7th; concentration +11)

7/day—*gentle rest*

**Inquisitor Spell-Like Abilities** (CL 7th; concentration +11)

At will—*detect alignment*, *discern lies* (7 rounds/day)

**Inquisitor Spells Known** (CL 7th; concentration +11)

3rd (2/day)—*halt undead* (DC 17), *searing light*

2nd (4/day)—*cure moderate wounds* (DC 16), *false life*, *flames of the faithful*[APG] (DC 16), *spiritual weapon*

1st (5/day)—*cure light wounds* (DC 15), *divine favor*, *hide from undead* (DC 15), *lend judgment*[UM] (DC 15), *wrath*[APG]

0 (at will)—*acid splash*, *brand*[APG] (DC 14), *detect magic*, *guidance*, *resistance*, *stabilize*

**Domain** Repose

### STATISTICS

**Str** 14, **Dex** 17, **Con** 17, **Int** 10, **Wis** 18, **Cha** 10

**Base Atk** +11; **CMB** +13; **CMD** 26

**Feats** Great Fortitude, Improved Two-Weapon Fighting, Iron Will, Lightning Reflexes, Precise Strike[APG], Shake It Off[UC], Two-Weapon Fighting, Weapon Finesse, Weapon Focus (dagger)

**Skills** Intimidate +19, Knowledge (religion) +16, Linguistics +1, Perception +20, Sense Motive +23, Stealth +24, Survival +13, Use Magic Device +9

**Languages** Abyssal, Celestial, Infernal, Nightsong (see above)

**SQ** death's dagger, ectoplasmic focus, monster lore +4, solo tactics, stern gaze +3, track +3

**Combat Gear** scrolls of ward the faithful[APG] (2); **Other Gear** *+1 shadow studded leather*, *+1 undead-bane returning daggers* (2), *belt of incredible dexterity +2*

inner sea temples

Sacred Spaces and Profane Places

Cathedral of Exquisite Agony

Cayden's Hall

First Colonial Bank of Sargava

High Temple of Pharasma

House of Dawn's Redemption

Imvrildara

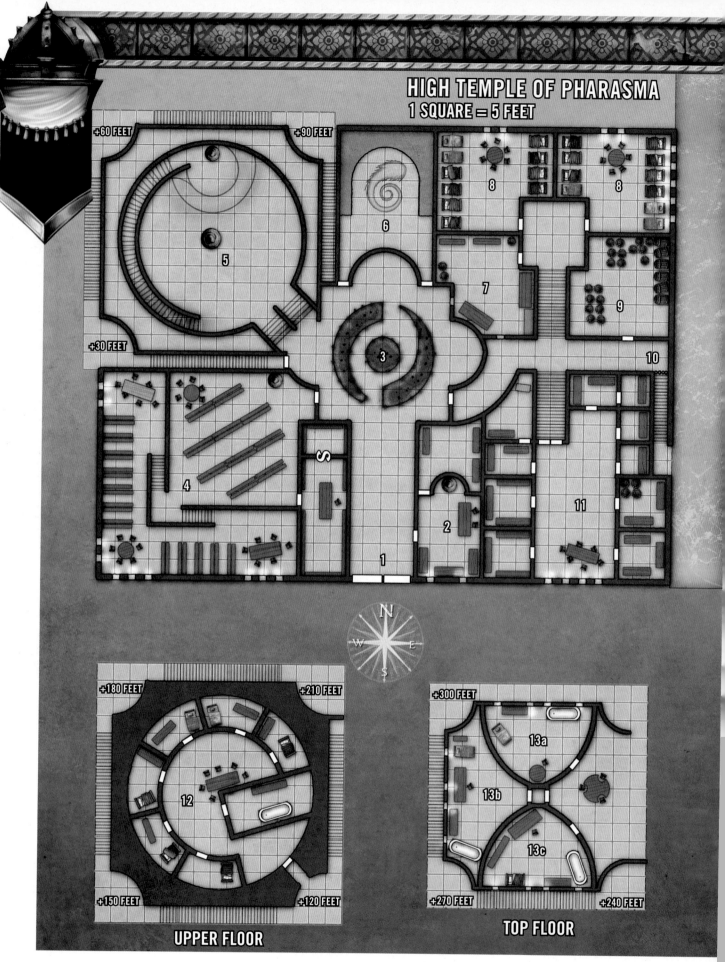

# HIGH TEMPLE OF PHARASMA
## 1 SQUARE = 5 FEET

+60 FEET

+90 FEET

5

6

8

8

7

9

+30 FEET

10

3

4

S

11

2

1

+180 FEET

+210 FEET

+300 FEET

13a

12

13b

13c

+150 FEET

+120 FEET

+270 FEET

+240 FEET

**UPPER FLOOR**

**TOP FLOOR**

N
W    E
S

# GAZETTEER

The High Temple of Pharasma is located on the eastern edge of the Necropolis of the Faithful, immediately adjacent to the Crimson Canal. Because the temple was built around the ancient Shrine of the Graves, from which the necropolis expanded outward to the north, west, and south, the age of the tombs and graves around it can be calculated quite accurately based on their distance from the temple. Those closest to the temple date back to the First Age of Ancient Osirion and the time of the first pharaohs.

## 1. Skull Gate (CR 4)

The High Temple's arched main gate is named for the skull-shaped keystone above it. Built from granite and black steel and reinforced with magic, the gate is opened each day at dawn, and barred from the inside at dusk (hardness 10, hp 60, break DC 30).

**Trap:** If the gate is forcibly opened, a permanent *symbol of healing* activates, damaging any undead creatures and healing the priests who rush to defend the gate.

| SYMBOL OF HEALING | CR 4 |
|---|---|
| **XP 1,200** | |

**Type** magic; **Perception** DC 28; **Disable Device** DC 28

**EFFECTS**

**Trigger** spell; **Duration** 140 minutes; **Reset** automatic
**Effect** spell effect (*symbol of healing*UM [CL 14th], 2d8+14 points of damage, Will DC 18 half); multiple targets (all targets within 60 feet)

## 2. Shrine of the Graves

The oldest structure in the High Temple of Pharasma, this chamber was originally the prayer room of the first Pharasmin church built on this site. Now the Shrine of the Graves is a shop stocked with holy items and religious souvenirs for pilgrims. According to the pale, deathly thin shopkeeper **Marikah Famedha** (NG female old human adept 4), the most popular souvenirs for sale are whippoorwill-shaped clay whistles (see page 42), tiny vials of holy water, necklaces shaped like scarab beetles, daggers, hourglasses, spirals, and skulls, as well as black roses treated with *preserve* (see page 43). These roses come from the temple's rosarium (area 3), and only a limited number of them are sold every year. Candles are also one of the temple's best-selling items; the faithful of Pharasma leave small candles on the temple's altar, and on the anniversary of the death of a loved one, they leave larger candles—also known as soul candles (see page 42)—on the graves.

## 3. Black Rosarium (CR 7)

The priests of the High Temple have cultivated roses on the temple grounds for millennia, a tradition that began when a Pharasmin cleric discovered a single bush bearing black roses growing in the necropolis. The priests nurtured the rosebush and planted a few stems near the Shrine of the Graves. Scholars speculate that a combination of the temple's proximity to the Crimson Canal and the large number of decaying bodies buried in the soil has created growing conditions perfect for these black roses, but the Pharasmins naturally maintain that the unique roses are a sign of Pharasma's favor.

The rose beds are situated behind a black wrought iron fence with beautiful spiraling patterns reminiscent of whippoorwills and iron roses with stems that are studded with sharp spikes to discourage visitors from reaching in to pluck the blossoms. The roses have a sweet, heady, and spicy scent that has relaxing qualities, and for this reason, priests often spend time in the rosarium in quiet contemplation. Every year, a species of Avistani whippoorwill migrates to northern Garund, and a few of dozen of these birds winter in the rosarium, feeding on insects and helping keep the roses healthy. At night, their haunting, ethereal song can be heard across the temple grounds.

**Creature:** On moonlit nights, a dark, robed figure can sometimes be seen studying the roses. This is Suruhuntu, a vanth psychopomp assigned to watch the procession of the departed souls from the necropolis to the Boneyard. Cold and uncaring, she rarely helps the priests of the temple directly, and then only when she must do so to perform her duties.

| SURUHUNTU | CR 7 |
|---|---|
| **XP 3,200** | |

Female vanth psychopomp (*Pathfinder RPG Bestiary 4* 221)
**hp** 76

## 4. Archives of the Sepulcher (CR 6)

One of the oldest extant libraries in Garund, though not the largest, the Archives of the Sepulcher hold an impressive corpus of holy texts. The most prized among them are a series of papyrus scrolls containing Pharasma's holy book, *The Bones Land in a Spiral*, written in Ancient Osiriani, but the collection includes translations of the book in nearly every language spoken on Golarion. The main purpose of the archives, however, is to preserve records about every person buried in the Necropolis of the Faithful, including the date and cause of death and a short account of the person's life, if known. The names and dates of birth of all children born to members of the church are similarly recorded here. The library's second floor contains many books about childbirth, divinations, embalming, and undead slaying.

Because of the many historical and esoteric texts stored in the archives, any character who spends 1d4 hours researching a topic in the library gains a +4 circumstance bonus on Knowledge (history, planes, or religion) checks and can attempt these checks untrained.

inner sea temples

Sacred Spaces and Profane Places

Cathedral of Exquisite Agony

Cayden's Hall

First Colonial Bank of Sargava

High Temple of Pharasma

House of Dawn's Redemption

Imvrildara

**Creatures:** Any visitor who wishes to study the temple's holy texts must visit the office of Head Archivist Avinia Talin, an unusually tall halfling with a constantly furrowed brow and long hair kept in a spiraling bun. Touching any of the documents without Avinia's permission angers the library's eternal guardian Akathet, a graven guardian who otherwise appears to be a statue depicting the library's founder.

| AKATHET | CR 5 |
|---|---|

**XP 1,600**

Graven guardian of Pharasma (*Pathfinder RPG Bestiary 3* 140)

**hp** 53

| AVINIA TALIN | CR 4 |
|---|---|

**XP 1,200**

Female halfling temple priest (see page 2 and the sidebar on page 36)

**hp** 31

**Treasure:** The temple's collection of divine spell scrolls is also housed on the second floor of the archives. Nearly all spells available to clerics are included and available for sale, except for spells expressly forbidden by the Pharasmin faith, such as *animate dead*. For research purposes, however, a few copies of such forbidden spells are stored in the head archivist's office, located just to the east of the archives, behind a secret door (Perception DC 20).

## 5. Shrine of the Red Sand

This chamber is the High Temple's central worship area. Pharasmin priests give sermons and perform rituals on a circular platform to the north, which serves as the temple's altar and holds a statue of the Lady of Graves seated on her bone throne. A 12-foot-tall hourglass stands on a pedestal in the center of the shrine. Red sand endlessly flows through the hourglass, and a magical light inside it illuminates the chamber with a dim red glow. The hourglass symbolizes continuity; although individual lives begin and end as fate dictates, future generations of the faithful remember their dead and carry on their legacy.

Bronze signs at the shrine's entrance, in both Osiriani and Taldane, urge visitors to enter using the stairs on the left and progress through the shrine in a clockwise direction, following the direction of Pharasma's spiraling symbol, and representing the acceptance of one's fate. The faithful usually make the Sign of the Lady (tracing a spiral in the air or over one's chest) before entering the shrine. Inside, supplicants kneel and pray for guidance and protection before the altar, often lighting candles and leaving offerings on the altar's lowest tier before departing the shrine.

## 6. Sacristy

Items used during religious services are stored in this sacristy, which features an inlaid holy symbol of Pharasma on the floor. Numerous silver chalices, brass censers filled with incense, vials of holy water, and other ecclesiastical items sit atop a large curved table.

**Treasure:** Drawers in the table hold dozens of *scrolls of bless*, *oils of gentle repose*, *oils of sanctify corpse*^UM, and *cure potions* of assorted strength.

## 7. Kitchen

Acolytes bake pita bread, cook fava bean stew, fry fish, and prepare other dishes for the temple's residents in this kitchen, but they must carry meals to the priests living in the Bone Spire before they are allowed to eat.

## 8. Dormitory (CR varies)

Acolytes sleep in these dormitories, usually retiring for the night around dusk and waking up 2 hours before dawn to make breakfast and prepare for a new day of work. The eastern dormitory has a view over the Crimson Canal, but the water reeks of sewage on hot summer days.

| TEMPLE PRIEST | CR 4 |
|---|---|

**XP 1,200**

**hp** 31 (see page 2 and the sidebar on page 36)

## 9. Warehouse

The barrels in the warehouse are full of foodstuffs such as beans, coffee, fish, olive oil, peas, salt, vegetables, and wheat flour.

## 10. Canal Gate

Due to the proximity of the Crimson Canal, the priests of the High Temple receive much of their food and other supplies by boat. A team of acolytes led by a priest carry the supplies to the adjacent warehouse (area 9). The ironbound door at the top of the stairs that lead down to the canal is usually locked (hardness 5, hp 20, break DC 25, Disable Device DC 30).

## 11. Nightjars' Lodge (CR 9)

Originally an armory for the High Temple's priests, this building was converted into a headquarters for the secretive Order of the Nightjar a century ago. The central area of the old armory serves as the Nightjars' training, meeting, and dining room. It's mostly quiet during the day, but at dusk, after visitors have left the temple grounds, the Nightjars begin their "day" by dining, praying together, and preparing their spells. After a brief break, they engage in a daily training routine, maintain their equipment, and prepare for their nightly mission. Around midnight, following a briefing by the orders' leaders, the Nightjars head out into the necropolis.

The storage rooms surrounding the central hall are stocked with various arms, shields, and suits of armor. The collection includes crossbows, daggers, maces, sickles, and spears.

**Creatures**: The Nightjars' leader, Sister **Enheruket** (N female elf warpriest[ACG] of Pharasma 11) believes that all undead should be ended as quickly as possible with no exceptions. Hundreds of undead creatures have met their ends at the hands of this albino elf, who adeptly wields a long silver elven curve blade. Her lieutenant, Brother **Jalala** (NG male human necromancer 10) firmly believes that destroying undead is an act of mercy, and has helped numerous haunts and undead creatures depart by righting the wrongs that kept their souls tied to the Material Plane, rather than just outright destroying them. Bolstered by his spells, this tall Garundi wizard fights just as fiercely as his more martial brethren, combining spells and attacks with his magical repeating crossbow, *Nightpiercer* (see page 42).

In addition, the Nightjars are assisted by the ahmuuth psychopomp Ta-Hepu. Armed with twin daggers and ever-present floating gravestone shields, the owl-masked Ta-Hepu does not join every nightly mission, but the other Nightjars welcome her presence and skill with her weapons whenever the psychopomp accompanies them into the necropolis.

| TA-HEPU | CR 9 |
| --- | --- |

**XP 6,400**

**hp** 110 (see page 37)

## 12. PRIESTS' QUARTERS

Fully ordained priests of the High Temple occupy private rooms on various levels inside the Bone Spire. The higher a priest's rank, the higher up the spire her quarters are located. An added benefit of attaining higher status is that the higher levels of the spire are more exposed to and thus better cooled by the wind. While proximity to the canal and the spire's light coloration help keep the rest of the building cool, temperatures can still get uncomfortably high in the summer months.

## 13. HIGH PRIESTS' CHAMBERS

The temple's three high priests live in the pyramidion at the very top of the Bone Spire. On most days, it is possible to see all of Sothis at once from the top. The northernmost room (area **13a**) belongs to High Priest **Anawati Meridah** (N female human oracle[APG] 11), a blind Mwangi woman who represents the birth aspect of the Pharasmin faith. Beyond her expertise as a midwife, it is said that Anawati can see glimpses of the future lives of all children born in Sothis. The eccentric High Priest **Mehomnet** (CN female old dwarf diviner 12), representing Pharasma's aspect of fate, lives in the western room (area **13b**). During her long life, she has predicted many catastrophic events that have occurred on Golarion, but just as many of her predictions have failed. The southern room (area **13c**) belongs to the High Temple's de facto leader, High Priest **Inebni Andebar** (NG male human cleric of Pharasma 14), a somber but kind Garundi man. He manages the church's finances, supervises all building projects, and organizes the temple's major religious festivals, as well as overseeing the Necropolis of the Faithful.

TA-HEPU

## PHARASMIN MAGIC

The following section details equipment, magic items, and spells favored by priests of the High Temple of Pharasma.

### PHARASMIN EQUIPMENT

The following items are favored by Pharasmin devotees, and are available for sale at the High Temple of Pharasma.

| CLAY WHIPPOORWILL | PRICE 5 GP |
|---|---|
| | WEIGHT 1/2 lb. |

In addition to being an instrument suitable for Perform (wind instruments) checks, this elaborately crafted whippoorwill-shaped clay ocarina also doubles the effective range of the secret whistled Nightsong language (see page 37) to a distance of 1,000 feet.

| SOUL CANDLE | PRICE 1 GP |
|---|---|
| | WEIGHT — |

When lit, this spiral-shaped candle burns for 24 hours, but if a haunt manifests or an undead creature comes within 5 feet of a lit soul candle, the candle goes out in a bright, sizzling flash.

### PHARASMIN MAGIC ITEMS

The following magic items help the priests of the High Temple keep the threat of undead at bay.

| NIGHTPIERCER | | PRICE 12,700 GP |
|---|---|---|
| SLOT wrists | CL 9th | WEIGHT 12 lbs. |
| AURA moderate conjuration | | |

This +1 repeating heavy crossbow is carved in the shape of a stylized whippoorwill; the stirrup resembles the head, the limbs look like the wings, and the stock is shaped like the bird's tail. Nightpiercer applies the ghost touch weapon special ability to all bolts fired from it, and the bolts shriek like whippoorwills as they fly through the air. Whenever a bolt fired from Nightpiercer deals damage to an incorporeal undead creature, the bolt remains embedded in the creature, reducing all of the target's speeds by half (to a minimum of 5 feet) for 1 round.

| CONSTRUCTION REQUIREMENTS | COST 6,700 GP |
|---|---|

Craft Magic Arms and Armor, dimensional anchor, plane shift

| RING OF THE FAITHFUL DEAD | | PRICE 1000 GP |
|---|---|---|
| SLOT ring | CL 3rd | WEIGHT — |
| AURA faint evocation | | |

This spiraling silver ring glows briefly when a living creature puts it on. If its wearer of a ring of the faithful dead is slain by a creature with the create spawn ability, the wearer does not rise as an undead creature, even if the ring is later removed. If a corpse is wearing a ring of the faithful dead, any attempts to create an undead creature from the corpse (such as via animate dead) automatically fail, though simply removing the ring ends this protection.

| CONSTRUCTION REQUIREMENTS | COST 500 GP |
|---|---|

Forge Ring, sanctify corpse[UM]

| STONE OF TOMB WARDING | | PRICE 5,000 GP |
|---|---|---|
| SLOT none | CL 3rd | WEIGHT 1 lb. |
| AURA faint necromancy | | |

When hung above a door or other portal, this smooth, scarab-shaped stone prevents undead creatures from entering. An intelligent undead creature attempting to move through the warded portal or touch the stone must attempt a DC 13 Will save. If it fails, the creature cannot make another attempt until 24 hours have passed. If it succeeds, the creature is immune to the stone's effect for 24 hours. Nonintelligent undead creatures don't get a saving throw against the effect.

| CONSTRUCTION REQUIREMENTS | COST 2,500 GP |
|---|---|

Craft Wondrous Item, command undead

### PHARASMIN SPELLS

The following spells help the priests of the High Temple perform their daily tasks and fight undead.

**FUNEREAL WEAPON**

**School** transmutation; **Level** cleric 1, inquisitor 1, occultist 1, paladin 1

**Casting Time** 1 standard action

**Components** V, S, DF

**Range** touch

**Target** weapon touched or 50 projectiles (all of which must be together at the time of casting)

**Duration** 1 minute/level

**Saving Throw** Will negates (harmless, object); **Spell Resistance** yes (harmless, object)

You imbue a weapon with a faint silvery glow that dimly illuminates a 5-foot square. An affected weapon also easily bypasses the physical defenses of undead creatures, ignoring 5 points of an undead creature's damage reduction, as long as the damage reduction is not DR/epic. For example, attacks with a weapon affected by this spell completely ignore a zombie's DR 5/slashing or reduce a lich's damage reduction to DR 10/bludgeoning and magic.

You can't cast this spell on a natural weapon, such as an unarmed strike. Funereal weapon affects the DR of only undead creatures.

**NECROSTASIS**

**School** necromancy; **Level** cleric 2, inquisitor 2, shaman 2, sorcerer/wizard 3, spiritualist 2, witch 2

**Casting Time** 1 standard action

**Components** V, S, M/DF (a finger bone)

**Range** close (25 ft. + 5 ft./2 levels)

**Target** one undead creature

**Duration** 1 round/level (D)

**Saving Throw** Will negates; **Spell Resistance** yes

You drain necromantic energy from an undead creature, inducing a sluggish stupor. The target becomes staggered. For the duration of the spell, dark wisps of energy seep out of the target creature. If the target already has the staggered condition (as a zombie does), it becomes dazed for 1 round instead.

## PRESERVE

**School** necromancy; **Level** adept 1, cleric 1, medium 1, occultist 1, ranger 1, shaman 1, sorcerer/wizard 1, spiritualist 1, witch 1
**Casting Time** 1 standard action
**Components** V, S, M/DF (a pinch of salt)
**Range** touch
**Target** one or more objects touched, up to 1 lb./level
**Duration** 1 week
**Saving Throw** Will negates (object); **Spell Resistance** yes (object)

You imbue one or more objects with magic that dramatically slows down natural processes that lead to decay and spoilage. For the duration of the spell, food, water, plants, and other perishable objects affected by the spell remain as fresh as they were when the spell was cast. The spell also protects these objects against spells of the same level or lower that cause spoilage, such as *putrefy food and drink*APG. When the duration of *preserve* expires, the objects resume aging at their normal rate.

The spell also works on severed body parts and the bodies of small creatures as per *gentle repose*, provided that the weight of the creature or part does not exceed the spell's limit.

*Preserve* can be made permanent with a *permanency* spell by a caster of 9th level or higher for 500 gp.

## SPIRAL ASCENT

**School** conjuration (teleportation); **Level** cleric 3, inquisitor 3
**Casting Time** 1 standard action
**Components** V, S
**Range** long (400 ft. + 40 ft./level)
**Target** you and touched objects
**Duration** instantaneous
**Saving Throw** Will negates (object); **Spell Resistance** yes (object)

You transform yourself into a helical beam of divine energy that instantly transports you upward to a spot within range. The destination must be a square in the spell's range that's within 10 feet of a point directly above you. The destination must be within your line of sight or familiar to you. After using this spell, you can't take any other actions until your next turn. You can bring along objects as long as their weight doesn't exceed your maximum load.

If you arrive in a place that is already occupied by a solid body, you are teleported to a random open space on a suitable surface within the range and other limitations of the spell. If no such space is available, the spell simply fails. This spell does not function on a plane lacking gravity. On a plane with subjective directional gravity, you can use this spell to teleport in any direction.

## SPIRAL DESCENT

**School** conjuration (teleportation); **Level** cleric 2, inquisitor 2
**Casting Time** 1 standard action
**Components** V, S
**Range** long (400 ft. + 40 ft./level)
**Target** you and touched objects
**Duration** instantaneous
**Saving Throw** Will negates (object); **Spell Resistance** yes (object)

This spell functions as *spiral ascent*, except the destination and direction of travel is downward from your current location.

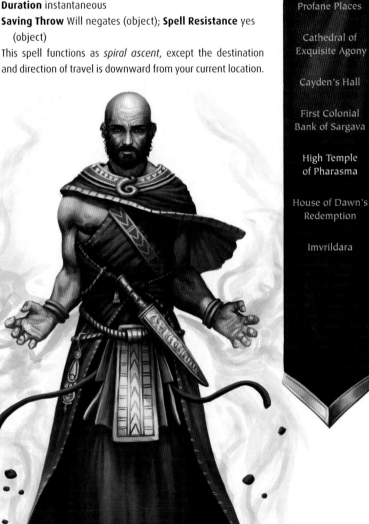

# HOUSE OF DAWN'S REDEMPTION

"The Gilded City is a splendid sight at any time of day, but never is it so magnificent than at dawn, when the first rays of the sun shine on the rose-gold domes of the House of Dawn's Redemption and the song of the Suncallers rings out over Oppara's rooftops from the temple's twin minarets. For those brief moments at the beginning of the day, I am filled with joy, and it is almost as if I had never left Katheer. Sarenrae's light shines on all the cities of the Inner Sea, from Corentyn to Katheer, but to me it seems to shine all the brighter in Oppara, as if the Dawnflower herself cannot contain her delight that her faith has returned to Taldor's shores, just as the sun rises every morning to banish the darkness of night."

—Bahij al-Ghadar, devout Sarenite

Rising from the ashes of its predecessor like the legendary phoenix, the House of Dawn's Redemption symbolizes the resurrection of Sarenrae's faith within Taldor, where worship of the Dawnflower was outlawed for a time. However, the roots of Sarenrae's church in Taldor run deep, and its return is more welcomed than opposed. Located in Taldor's capital, Oppara, the House of Dawn's Redemption is now the most prominent temple of Sarenrae in that nation.

Rivaling the splendor of Oppara's other religious landmark, the ancient Basilica of the Last Man, the House of Dawn's Redemption's Qadiran architecture is an exotic counterpoint to the traditional Taldan style that dominates the capital, as if the temple had been magically transported from the distant city of Katheer. Twelve rose-gold domes sparkle in the sunlight above the stout whitewashed wall that surrounds the temple, enclosing a grand, tiled courtyard lined with countless cerulean blue ceramic tiles. Two stylized minarets tower above the

courtyard and its starburst-shaped fountains. Thousands of blue ceramic tiles in varying hues adorn every inch of the temple's interior walls, while dizzying sunburst patterns of gold-and-white tiles decorate the interiors of the awe-inspiring domes.

## HISTORY

Just under 2 centuries ago, Sarenrae's faith flourished in Taldor, but the Keleshite origin of her church, and its long connection with Taldor's traditional rival, the nation of Qadira, created a perfect scapegoat for Taldor's political aims. Claiming that Sarenrae's followers, especially the militant Cult of the Dawnflower sect, could potentially open the doors for another Qadiran invasion of Taldor, Grand Prince Stavian I outlawed the worship of Sarenrae in Taldor in 4528 AR. Within months, nearly every Sarenite temple in Taldor was destroyed, and the Dawnflower's priests and followers were murdered or expelled in what came to be known as the Great Purge.

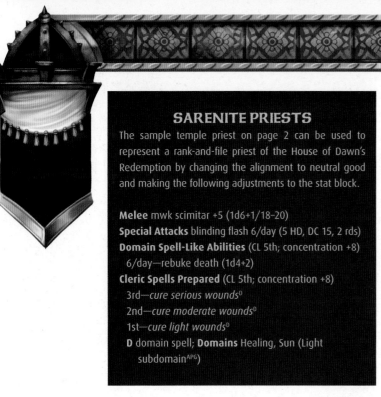

But just as the sun itself can never be extinguished, neither could Sarenrae's Taldan devotees completely abandon their faith. Carefully hidden within the general populace, faithful followers still gathered, secretly disseminating the Dawnflower's gospel and tenets while living in constant fear of persecution. Over the years, a covert sect flourished amid the very populace that had sought to drive them out. Secret signs, specialized whirling dances, flying doves, and sunflowers for sale at local markets all signaled the times and locations of secret worship services. While no official temple of Sarenrae existed in Oppara, the worship of the Healing Light prospered nonetheless. With each passing decade, Sarenrae's church grew, and Taldor's politics changed along with it.

Eventually, the Taldan government softened its stance against the Dawnflower; to atone for the injustices of the Great Purge, the city of Oppara returned to the church the same plot of land where Sarenrae's original temple once stood. Over the next decade, devoted Sarenites reclaimed the sacred sites of their goddess throughout Taldor, and many sanctified stones and lost relics were brought to Oppara to rebuild a new cathedral atop the ashes of the old razed temple. Rather than focus on the wrongs they endured, Sarenrae's faithful instead built a center for healing and forgiveness called the House of Dawn's Redemption. Today, this bright beacon to the Dawnflower stands as a shining symbol of the return of Sarenrae's faith to Taldor.

## ORGANIZATION

Sarenrae's clergy is broad and diverse, with clerics, bards, paladins, and others serving as priests. The high priest of a Sarenite temple is called the Dawnfather or Dawnmother, and the post is usually held by a wise and revered elder learned in the skills of diplomacy and healing. Through years of devoted service, great deeds, and zeal for the

Cleansing Light, any priest can eventually ascend to the position, which is usually elected by the temple's congregation when the previous high priest relinquishes his post, either through retirement or death. At the House of Dawn's Redemption, it is not uncommon for a Dawnfather or Dawnmother to willingly abdicate the post to a younger candidate who has proven her worth and devotion. Despite the obvious Keleshite influences of the temple, most of the clergy of the House of Dawn's Redemption are themselves Taldan. As is common in Sarenrae's faith (though not in Taldor as a whole), priests at the House of Dawn's Redemption wear vestments decorated with sunbursts, patterned after the robes of Keleshite desert nomads, and usually carry scimitars, the favored weapon of their goddess.

In addition to its ordained clergy, the House of Dawn's Redemption hosts a sect of Dawnflower dervishes, elegant warriors garbed in pure white who are quick to defend the temple when threatened, dancing and whirling across the battlefield and slicing through their foes with razor-sharp scimitars. Some of these dervishes hold the rank of Suncaller and sound the dawn call to prayer.

## MEMBERSHIP AND RELATIONS

Membership in Sarenrae's faith is open to all; even villains who have found redemption are free to join the flock as equals under the Cleansing Light. Most of the House of Dawn's Redemption's congregation are Taldan, not Keleshite. Members of the church (and those doing business in the Dawnflower Market) are expected to tithe a small portion of their livelihood or profits to the temple, and those who do can benefit from the church's healing services and social networking. The faithful are encouraged to keep their right hands clean, as this is the hand offered for healing others and must remain as sterile as possible to stave off infections and other calamities.

Adventurers, especially those with heroic hearts, are most welcome at the House of Dawn's Redemption, as these individuals often represent the ideals of the Dawnflower. Successful adventurers who display devotion and generosity toward the temple and its congregation enjoy significant discounts on the purchase of the church's healing services in return for their great deeds.

Relatively new to Oppara, the House of Dawn's Redemption is still looked upon with suspicion by those with long memories of the Qadiran occupation. The temple has, at times, been a target of vandalism by those who oppose the church's renewed presence in Taldor, but the faithful believe Sarenrae's message of honesty and redemption applies to themselves as well, and many see the House of Dawn's Redemption as a symbol of the Dawnflower's long overdue return to Taldor.

## NOTABLE DENIZENS

The most prominent inhabitant of the House of Dawn's Redemption is the temple's high priestess, Dawnmother Zenaida Tandleos. A native Taldan, she has held the post for over 25 years. She has dedicated her life to the healing arts and is committed to promoting Sarenrae's creed of kindness, honesty, and redemption.

| ZENAIDA TANDLEOS | CR 8 |
|---|---|

**XP 4,800**

Female middle-aged human cleric of Sarenrae 9

NG Medium humanoid (human)

**Init** +3; **Senses** Perception +5

**Aura** divine presence (30 ft., DC 19, 9 rounds/day)

**DEFENSE**

**AC** 9, touch 9, flat-footed 9 (–1 Dex)

**hp** 62 (9d8+18)

**Fort** +8, **Ref** +3, **Will** +12

**OFFENSE**

**Speed** 30 ft.

**Melee** *+1 scimitar* +5/+0 (1d6–1/18–20)

**Special Attacks** channel positive energy 8/day (DC 17 [19 to damage undead], 5d6)

**Domain Spell-Like Abilities** (CL 9th; concentration +14)

8/day—rebuke death (1d4+4), touch of glory (+9)

**Cleric Spells Prepared** (CL 9th; concentration +14)

5th—*breath of life*[D], *flame strike* (DC 20), *pillar of life*[APG]

4th—*cure critical wounds*[D], *neutralize poison*, *restoration*, *tongues*

3rd—*cure serious wounds*[D], *dispel magic*, *flame blade*, *remove blindness/deafness*, *symbol of healing*[UM]

2nd—*calm emotions*, *cure moderate wounds*[D], *instant armor*[APG], *lesser restoration*, *spiritual weapon*, *status*

1st—*bless*, *diagnose disease*[UM], *protection from evil*, *remove fear*, *remove sickness*[UM], *shield of faith*[D], *sun metal*[UC]

0 (at will)—*detect magic*, *detect poison*, *light*, *stabilize*

**D** domain spell; **Domains** Glory, Healing

**STATISTICS**

**Str** 7, **Dex** 9, **Con** 12, **Int** 14, **Wis** 20, **Cha** 16

**Base Atk** +6; **CMB** +4; **CMD** 13

**Feats** Combat Expertise, Extra Channel, Improved Initiative, Merciful Spell[APG], Quick Channel[UM], Skill Focus (Heal)

**Skills** Diplomacy +15, Handle Animal +8, Heal +22, Knowledge (history) +8, Knowledge (religion) +14, Profession (herbalist) +9, Sense Motive +17

**Languages** Celestial, Common, Kelish

**SQ** healer's blessing

**Combat Gear** *bandages of rapid recovery*[UE], *potions of cure light wounds* (2), *scroll of heal*; **Other Gear** *+1 scimitar*, *cloak of resistance +1*, *headband of inspired wisdom +2*, cleric's vestments, golden holy symbol of Sarenrae (worth 100 gp), healer's kit, spell component pouch, diamond dust (worth 100 gp), powdered diamond and opal (worth 500 gp), 25 gp

innersea temples

Sacred Spaces and Profane Places

Cathedral of Exquisite Agony

Cayden's Hall

First Colonial Bank of Sargava

High Temple of Pharasma

House of Dawn's Redemption

Imvrildara

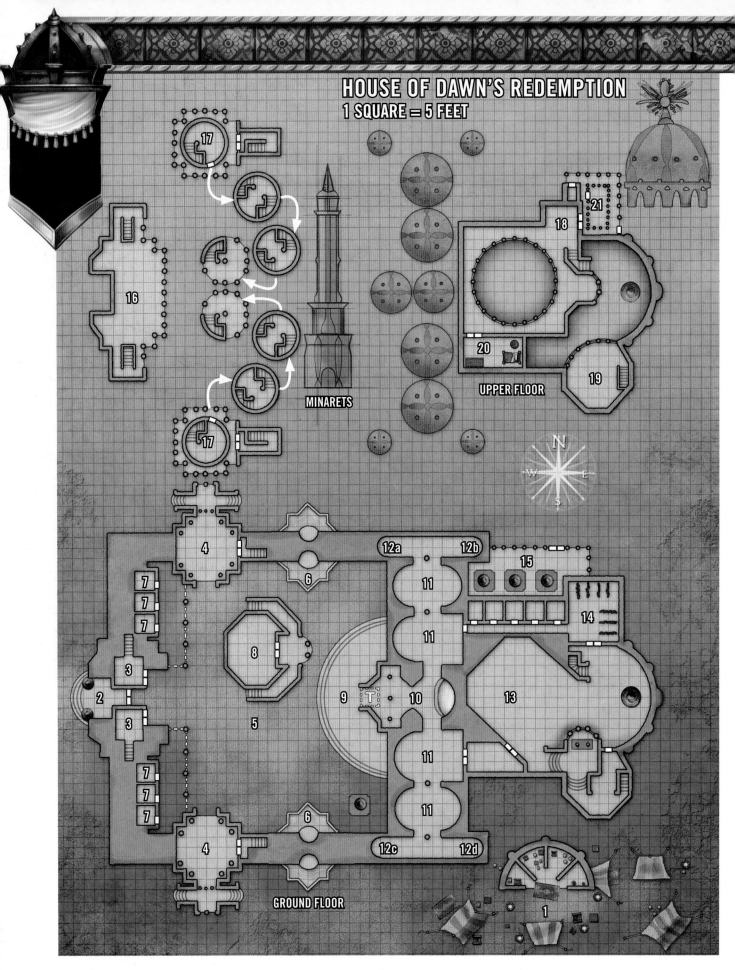

# HOUSE OF DAWN'S REDEMPTION
## 1 SQUARE = 5 FEET

17

16

17

MINARETS

18

21

20

19

UPPER FLOOR

N
W E
S

4

7
7
7

3

2

3

7
7
7

4

GROUND FLOOR

8

5

6

6

9

T

10

5

12a

12b

11

11

11

11

12c

12d

13

15

14

1

# GAZETTEER

The House of Dawn's Redemption proudly stands in the heart of Oppara's Grandbridge district, a bustling mercantile neighborhood that hosts visitors from around the world. The temple's dozen rose-gold domes and twin minarets catch the rays of both the rising and setting sun, and the dawn call to prayer echoes daily over the neighboring districts.

## 1. Dawnflower Market

A lively, Qadiran-style market sits just outside the temple walls. The wooden stalls, canvas tents, and horse carts sell all manner of church paraphernalia, jewelry, pottery, and spices, as well as a myriad of healing balms and salves of varying efficacy. Traditionally, transactions are sealed over a cup of the market's famous sunflower tea.

## 2. Dusk Gate

The main entrance to the House of Dawn's Redemption faces the direction of the setting sun. Statues depicting two of Sarenrae's celestial servitors flank an iron double door, which is closed and locked at sunset every night (hardness 10, hp 60, break DC 28, Disable Device DC 30).

## 3. Guardroom (CR 6)

These rooms permanently house the temple's guards. Each room contains a steep staircase providing access to the gatehouse roof (area 16).

**Creatures:** Four temple guards, two in each guardroom, guard the Dusk Gate (area 2).

| TEMPLE GUARDS (4) | CR 2 |
|---|---|

**XP 600 each**
NG veteran buccaneer (*Pathfinder RPG NPC Codex* 267)
**hp** 26 each

## 4. Minaret Gate

These two side gates are located beneath the temple's twin minarets. At sunset, a heavy portcullis is lowered to block each gate (hardness 10, hp 60, lift DC 25). A small room to the east of each gate contains a staircase that leads to the minarets above (area 17).

## 5. Courtyard

Surrounded by a thick, whitewashed wall, the temple's central courtyard is paved with thousand of blue ceramic tiles, each baked under the Qadiran sun. Open-air worship services beneath the sun are held in the courtyard, where the faithful also gather before and after services.

## 6. Ablution Fountain (CR 7)

Visitors to the House of Dawn's Redemption are expected to ceremonially cleanse themselves in either of these two starburst-shaped fountains when they first enter the temple. Awareness of this Keleshite tradition requires a successful DC 15 Knowledge (local or religion) check. Anyone failing to wash themselves before entering the temple proper (areas 10 through 14) takes a –2 penalty on Bluff, Diplomacy, Disguise, Perform, and Stealth checks within the temple.

**Creatures:** A pair of playful celestial water mephits inhabits each fountain. They are prone to performing harmless pranks on newcomers, but come to the temple's defense when necessary. Instead of their *stinking cloud* spell-like ability, these mephits can cast *create water* at will.

| MISCHIEVOUS MEPHITS (4) | CR 3 |
|---|---|

**XP 800 each**
NG variant celestial water mephit (*Pathfinder RPG Bestiary* 294, 202)
**hp** 19 each
**Spell-Like Abilities**
At will—*create water*

## 7. Priest Cells (CR 4)

Each of these six modest chambers contains a simple cot.

**Creatures:** Each cell houses one of the temple's junior priests, who spend their downtime sitting or kneeling on simple prayer mats while studying the tenets of the Dawnflower's faith.

| TEMPLE PRIESTS (6) | CR 4 |
|---|---|

**XP 1,200 each**
**hp** 31 each (see page 2 and the sidebar on page 46)

## 8. Dervish House (CR varies)

Tiled in scintillating swirls of fiery oranges, reds, and yellows, this octagonal building provides a striking contrast to the sea of blue tiles found elsewhere in the courtyard. Inside, several astrological markings decorate the floor. A character who succeeds at a DC 15 Knowledge (nature) check identifies this pattern as a celestial map of the sun's travels around the solar system. Furthermore, a successful DC 20 Knowledge (arcana) or Perform (dance) check reveals that the swirling motion of the sun's charted path can be traversed in a whirling dance. If anyone can perform the complicated steps to recreate the sun's journey through the heavens—which requires a successful DC 30 Perform (dance) check—the vigorous spinning dance induces a trancelike state that lasts for 8 days. During this time, a ghostly dervish teaches the character an occult ritual known as the dance of the Dawnflower dervish (see page 53).

**Creatures:** The temple's contingent of dervishes dwells in the Dervish House. At any given time, 1d6 temple dervishes can be found in residence here. These dervishes have ranks in Perform (dance) instead of Perform (string) and wield masterwork scimitars rather than rapiers.

innersea
temples

Sacred Spaces
and
Profane Places

Cathedral of
Exquisite Agony

Cayden's Hall

First Colonial
Bank of Sargava

High Temple
of Pharasma

House of Dawn's
Redemption

Imvrildara

**XP 1,600 each**
NG minstrel (*Pathfinder RPG GameMastery Guide* 273)
**hp** 30 each

## 9. Steps of the Fallen

These crumbling, fire-blackened marble steps stand in stark contrast to the pristine conditions found elsewhere within the temple grounds. Part of the original church that was razed years ago during the Great Purge, the stairs have been left unrepaired and unaltered as a memorial to the heroes who died trying to save the temple, and as a reminder of the hardships faced by the cult of the Dawnflower in the past.

## 10. Entry Hall (CR 6)

Visitors are required to remove their footwear before entering the temple, placing them in one of hundreds of small niches in the chamber's walls. A successful DC 15 Knowledge (local or religion) check is sufficient to know this practice. Anyone entering the rooms beyond with footwear is met with disapproval and firmly reminded to remove such accoutrements. Those who fail to do so are politely asked to leave, and risk raising the ire of the temple's guards if they still pay no heed.

A large basin to the east holds pure sunflower seed oil the color of daffodils. Worshipers anoint their faces and heads with this blessed oil, and anyone so anointed gains a +1 resistance bonus on saving throws against disease for 24 hours.

**Trap:** If the temple is threatened, a large, heated stone block can be rigged to drop down and seal this entry.

**HEATED FALLING BLOCK TRAP       CR 6**
**XP 2,400**
**Type** mechanical; **Perception** DC 20;
   **Disable Device** DC 20

**EFFECTS**

**Trigger** location; **Reset** manual
**Effect** Atk +15 melee (6d6 plus 2d4
   fire damage); multiple targets
   (all targets in a 10-ft. square)

## 11. Congregation Hall

Worshipers gather in these spaces to discuss matters of daily life, conduct honest business transactions, or even swear oaths of love before entering the prayer hall beyond (area **13**). Priests mingle with the congregation in these halls as well, encouraging community and mirth, and inquiring about the health and well-being of absent members of the faith.

## 12. Relics of the Faith

Decorative alcoves in these two chambers hold the House of Dawn's Redemption's most prized relics (see Treasure below), sealed behind alchemically treated glass (hardness 5, hp 20, break DC 23). If the glass is tampered with or broken, an audible alarm rings out, as per *alarm*.

**Hazard:** If any of the relics are removed from the temple without the permission of Dawnmother Zenaida Tandelos, the thief is subject to the relic robber's curse.

**RELIC ROBBER'S CURSE**

**Type** curse; **Save** Will DC 20 negates
  **Frequency** 1/day
   **Effect** The target develops an unhealthy obsession
    with the stolen relic, and all other possessions
    that the target owns seem worthless. Each day,
    the target is compelled to sell off its remaining
    possessions. Unless the target succeeds at a
    DC 20 Will save, it attempts to sell all of its
    gear to the nearest peddler at a 50%
    discount. The curse is automatically
    lifted if the target returns the
    stolen relic to the House of
    Dawn's Redemption and begs
    for forgiveness.

**Treasure:** The following relics are stored in these chambers: the *scabbard of the Lost Kiss* (area **12a**), a *dervish sikke* (area **12b**), *Sunlord's feather* (area **12c**), and the *Saliharion* (area **12d**). See page 52 for full descriptions of these items. In addition, each of the relics is warded by a curse (see Hazard above).

## 13. Prayer Hall (CR 8)

Thick carpets imported from Katheer line the floor of this barren chamber, where worshipers sit or kneel while they pay their respects to Sarenrae during worship services. To the east, a colossal bronze statue of Sarenrae stands in front of a beautiful glass tile mosaic depicting the Dawnflower's titanic

ZENAIDA TANDELOS

struggle with the Rough Beast, Rovagug. To the south, a raised teakwood platform called a minbar stands 10 feet above the floor, providing a podium for the priests to recite prayers and sermons and lead services. Past the minbar to the southeast is a small chamber used as a vestry. Stairs in the vestry climb to the choir loft (area **19**); another set of stairs to the north provides access to the Gallery of Mirrors (area **18**).

**Creature:** The tiled figure of Sarenrae in the mosaic on the eastern wall is actually a stained-glass golem that can detach from the wall to defend the temple in times of need.

| STAINED-GLASS GOLEM | CR 8 |
|---|---|

**XP 4,800**
Variant glass golem (*Pathfinder RPG Bestiary 2* 138)
**hp** 96

**Treasure:** The temple's magical *altar of the Dawnflower* (see page 52) sits atop the minbar.

## 14. Hospital (CR varies)

Priests and healers provide medical aid to both devout Sarenites and non-worshipers in this collection of rooms. Curtains divide the large chamber to the east into smaller bays with cots for emergency healing and surgery, while the five private hospice chambers to the west have beds and are reserved for long-term care of patients.

**Creatures:** Usually, 1d3 lay healers can be found on duty in the hospital, day or night.

| LAY HEALERS (1D3) | CR 3 |
|---|---|

**XP 800 each**
Pilgrim (*Pathfinder RPG GameMastery Guide* 291)
**hp** 17 each

**Treasure:** The following healing items can be found in the hospital: an antidote kit[UE], a chirurgeon's kit[UE], a healer's kit[UE], a leeching kit[UE], a midwife's kit[UE], a shaving kit[UE], and a set of masterwork surgeon's tools[UE].

## 15. Sunflower Cemetery

A wrought-iron fence encloses this small, sunflower-choked graveyard, where the faithful are interred beneath the light of the sun. The gate is usually kept unlocked during the day.

## 16. Gatehouse Roof

Situated above the Dusk Gate (area **2**), this rooftop is used by temple guards for defense or by priests to address crowds of the faithful in the courtyard below. A low wall provides partial cover against attacks from the west, while a grand balcony provides a splendid view of the courtyard (area **5**) to the east.

## 17. Minarets (CR 5)

These two hollow towers are 75 feet tall. Spiraling stairs inside the minarets climb to a balcony at the very top of each spire. A mechanism in the base of each tower controls the portcullis in the minaret gate below (area **4**).

**Creatures:** Two temple dervishes perform the dawn call to prayer from the gallery atop each minaret. Given the honorary title of Suncallers, these dervishes also act as sentries for the city of Oppara, keeping a sharp lookout for threats such as natural disasters or approaching invaders. They are identical to the dervishes in area **8**.

| TEMPLE DERVISHES (2) | CR 5 |
|---|---|

**XP 1,600 each**
NG minstrel (*Pathfinder RPG GameMastery Guide* 273)
**hp** 30 each

## 18. Gallery of Mirrors

Several brass mirrors stand at precise positions in this open room to redirect sunlight throughout the temple via a system of smaller mirrors. The gallery also provides magnificent views of the prayer hall (area **13**) and bronze statue of Sarenrae below.

## 19. Choir Loft

This balcony overlooks the prayer hall (area **13**) and provides space for a choir of singers and musicians to perform for the congregation and accompany worship services. An oversized zither-like instrument called a kanun and an assortment of Qadiran lutes are kept here for the choir's use.

## 20. Dawnmother's Chamber (CR 8)

This modest room serves as the private quarters of the high priestess of the House of Dawn's Redemption.

**Creature:** Dawnmother Zenaida Tandleos sleeps here, though she is more likely to be found mingling with congregants in the courtyard (area **5**), leading worship services in the prayer hall (area **13**), or tending to the sick in the temple's hospital (area **14**).

| ZENAIDA TANDLEOS | CR 8 |
|---|---|

**XP 4,800**
**hp** 62 (see page 47)

## 21. Aviary

This enclosure holds scores of doves that the temple uses for a variety of tasks, including delivering messages, singing, and sounding alarms. Due to its unique breeding, each dove grants its owner a +2 competence bonus on Handle Animal checks with the bird. In addition, a spellcaster can select one of these doves as a familiar. Use the statistics for a thrush (*Pathfinder RPG Ultimate Magic* 120); a dove's master gains a +3 bonus on Perform checks as a special ability.

innersea temples

Sacred Spaces and Profane Places

Cathedral of Exquisite Agony

Cayden's Hall

First Colonial Bank of Sargava

High Temple of Pharasma

House of Dawn's Redemption

Imvrildara

# SARENITE MAGIC

The following section details magic items and a ritual favored by the priests and dervishes of the House of Dawn's Redemption.

## SARENITE MAGIC ITEMS

The House of Dawn's Redemption has amassed an impressive collection of Sarenite relics, including the magical altar of the original Opparan temple. In times of need, the Dawnmother might loan one or more of the following magic items to noble adventurers who perform services in the name of Sarenrae.

| ALTAR OF THE DAWNFLOWER | | PRICE 10,000 GP |
|---|---|---|
| **SLOT** none | **CL** 10th | **WEIGHT** 250 lbs. |
| **AURA** moderate conjuration and enchantment [good, healing] | | |

Unearthed from the ashes of Oppara's former temple of Sarenrae, the restored and rededicated *altar of the Dawnflower* sits inside the House of Dawn's Redemption at the exact location it resided nearly 200 years ago. As a gift to welcome Sarenrae's faith back into Taldor, this reclaimed treasure symbolizes the hope for a peaceful existence between the traditionalists of Oppara and those longing for the light of the Healing Flame.

This altar consists of a tiled blue box detailed with mosaics of doves in flight. A stand for a scimitar is built on top of the altar. During important worship services, the *scabbard of the Lost Kiss* (see below) is often placed atop the altar's scimitar stand. Praying at the altar grants a +3 bonus on Diplomacy checks to redeem an evil creature or change the attitude of a creature opposed to the Sarenite faith. Creatures who rest or receive long-term care (with the Heal skill) within 60 feet of the altar also regain 1 additional hit point per level each day.

| CONSTRUCTION REQUIREMENTS | COST 5,000 GP |
|---|---|

Craft Wondrous Item, *cure light wounds*, *eagle's splendor*, *magic circle against evil*, creator must worship Sarenrae

| DERVISH SIKKE | | PRICE 10,000 GP |
|---|---|---|
| **SLOT** head | **CL** 10th | **WEIGHT** 1 lb. |
| **AURA** moderate transmutation | | |

This cylindrical felt hat, favored by Dawnflower dervishes, grants its wearer a +2 competence bonus on one Knowledge or Perform skill, chosen when the *dervish sikke* is created. Most *dervish sikkes* grant bonuses on Knowledge (religion) or Perform (dance) checks.

If the wearer is a bard, he is considered 5 class levels higher for purposes of determining the effects of his bardic knowledge class feature. In addition, the bonuses granted by a bard's inspire courage and inspire competence class features are increased by 1. Finally, a bard wearing a *dervish sikke* can take 10 on any Perform skill check he has ranks in.

| CONSTRUCTION REQUIREMENTS | COST 5,000 GP |
|---|---|

Craft Wondrous Item, *fox's cunning*, *timely inspiration*[APG]

| SALIHARION | | PRICE 3,000 GP |
|---|---|---|
| **SLOT** none | **CL** 5th | **WEIGHT** 15 lbs. |
| **AURA** faint divination | | |

Named for Nashina aj-Salihar, the Sarenite monk who penned the original work, this hefty tome contains inspiring parables, simple folk remedies for widespread illnesses and injuries, and helpful hints for dealing with common monsters. Its pages are expertly illuminated with brilliant inks and metallic foil, depicting scenes of angels battling various monstrosities. While in possession of this book, the owner gains a +2 sacred bonus on Heal checks and Knowledge skill checks to identify the abilities and weaknesses of monsters.

If Sarenrae is the owner's patron, the owner may instead choose to gain a sacred bonus equal to her Wisdom or Charisma modifier on these skill checks instead of the normal +2 bonus.

| CONSTRUCTION REQUIREMENTS | COST 1,500 GP |
|---|---|

Craft Wondrous Item, *know the enemy*[UM], *owl's wisdom*

| SCABBARD OF THE LOST KISS | | PRICE 8,600 GP |
|---|---|---|
| **SLOT** none | **CL** 4th | **WEIGHT** 1 lb. |
| **AURA** faint evocation | | |

This aged and worn scabbard is believed to have once held one of a dozen legendary scimitar relics named *Dawnflower's Kiss*. From its prolonged proximity to such a divine blade, the scabbard has acquired its own unique magical abilities. Twice per day on command, the wearer can draw forth a blazing beam of red-hot fire from the scabbard that can be wielded as if it were a scimitar, as per *flame blade*.

If Sarenrae is the wearer's patron, half of the *flame blade's* damage is fire damage, but the other half results directly from divine power and is therefore not subject to being reduced by resistance to fire.

| CONSTRUCTION REQUIREMENTS | COST 4,300 GP |
|---|---|

Craft Wondrous Item, *flame blade*, *flame strike*

| SUNLORD'S FEATHER | | PRICE 1,100 GP |
|---|---|---|
| **SLOT** none | **CL** 10th | **WEIGHT** — |
| **AURA** moderate transmutation | | |

Named after Sarenrae's herald, Sunlord Thalachos, this *+1 flaming holy arrow* has a platinum arrowhead and brilliant white fletching. When the arrow successfully strikes an evil-aligned creature, it explodes in a shower of golden sparks that summons a swarm of celestial doves (treat as a celestial bat swarm; *Pathfinder RPG Bestiary* 294, 30) that continues to attack the arrow's target for 10 rounds or until destroyed or dismissed. If the target is slain before the duration expires, the remaining doves fly off into the horizon.

| CONSTRUCTION REQUIREMENTS | COST 550 GP |
|---|---|

Craft Magic Arms and Armor, *flame strike*, *holy smite*, *summon swarm*, creator must be good

## SARENITE OCCULT RITUAL

The famous Dawnflower dervishes inspire both awe and fear in those who witness their elegant, ritualistic spinning dance and whirling fighting style. With years of practice, these holy warriors can enter a trance and perform the following occult ritual that mystically bolsters their already formidable fighting prowess. More information about occult rituals can be found on page 208 of *Pathfinder RPG Occult Adventures*.

### DANCE OF THE DAWNFLOWER DERVISH

**School** transmutation; **Level** 8

**Casting Time** 80 minutes

**Components** V, M (a flask of blessed sunflower seed oil worth 100 gp for each caster and a *potion of cat's grace*), F (a masterwork scimitar made from rose gold worth 5,000 gp), SC (at least 1, up to the Charisma modifier of the primary caster)

**Skill Checks** Acrobatics DC 30, 3 successes; Knowledge (religion) DC 30, 2 successes; Perform (dance) DC 30, 3 successes

**Range** touch

**Target** primary and secondary casters

**Duration** 1 day (D)

**Saving Throw** Will negates (harmless); **SR** yes (harmless)

**Backlash** The primary caster takes 2d6 points of damage and all casters are exhausted.

**Failure** All casters cannot be targeted by any beneficial spells from the conjuration (healing) school (such as *cure light wounds*) and cannot touch a scimitar for 1 year (this is a curse effect, and can be removed with *remove curse* or similar effects).

### EFFECT

This ritual must be cast at dawn beneath the open sky on the Material Plane. The ritual must be performed at a site of Sarenite worship (such as a dervish house, shrine, or temple of Sarenrae) that has hosted active worship services for at least 52 consecutive weeks. The primary caster holds aloft the rose-gold scimitar, and the secondary casters stand around him and begin spinning in place. The primary caster recites 23 verses from Sarenrae's holy text, *The Birth of Light and Truth*, taking a sip from the *potion of cat's grace* between each stanza. After the last verse is completed, the secondary casters whirl around the primary caster, each anointing the rose-gold scimitar with blessed sunflower seed oil. Upon the successful completion of the ritual, all the casters are filled with the spirits of dervish heroes, becoming faster, stronger, tougher, and more skilled in combat. Each caster gains a +4 enhancement bonus to Strength, Dexterity, and Constitution; a +2 dodge bonus to AC; and a +2 sacred bonus on all saving throws. The caster's base attack bonus is equal his character level (which may give the caster multiple attacks). If the caster's base attack bonus is already equal to his character level, he gains one additional attack at his highest base attack bonus when making a full-attack action. In addition, any scimitar wielded by a caster is treated as if it has the *keen* weapon special ability. In exchange, each caster temporarily loses his ability to cast spells, save for those from the conjuration (healing) school.

Finally, once during the duration of the ritual, each caster can activate a whirling dance on the battlefield as a standard action. While dancing, the caster gains the effects of a *displacement* spell and can use the Spring Attack and Whirlwind Attack feats as if he possessed them without meeting their prerequisites. This dance is a supernatural effect and lasts a number of rounds equal to the primary caster's character level.

Each caster of the ritual can individually choose to dismiss the ritual's effects for himself.

**innersea temples**

Sacred Spaces and Profane Places

Cathedral of Exquisite Agony

Cayden's Hall

First Colonial Bank of Sargava

High Temple of Pharasma

House of Dawn's Redemption

Imvrildara

# IMVRILDARA

It is a dark and treacherous place, as befitting the Savored Sting—a dark and treacherous goddess. The building is ancient, and though its walls remain strong there are clear signs of the many demonic assaults it has withstood. Despite this, the building is full of pleasant scents. The vines often smell powerfully of flowers, even when they show no sign of blooming, and there is an undertone of sharp, sweet honey in every room. There is art of the highest quality in nearly every chamber, but it often depicts visions I would prefer not to witness. I found myself relieved when the Imvrildarai suggested I need not make the trip to their stronghold in person for future communications.

—From a report to the Iadaran court

Nestled within the southern reaches of Kyonin's Fierani Forest, the Calistrian temple of Imvrildara stands as a testament to the ancient history of Calistria's worship and the Savored Sting's influence as the goddess of trickery and revenge. It is home to the Imvrildarai, a militant arm of the Calistrian faith devoted to the reclamation of that forest and the defeat of the demon lord Treerazer at any cost.

## HISTORY

Construction on Imvrildara was completed in –5570 AR at the behest of an unknown former sovereign of Kyonin. Imvrildara was intended to serve as a hub of the Calistrian faith in Kyonin, and was centrally located in what was once a considerably larger kingdom. The temple gained its name from an elven priest of Calistria who penned an illuminated manuscript chronicling the battle with Rovagug at the dawn of time, highlighting Calistria's participation in this mythic confrontation.

Imvrildara's focus on the battle against Treerazer began in 2497 AR, when elven refugees fleeing his incursion sought refuge in the temple. One of these refugees, a farmer by the name of Alendeil, became a priest of Calistria, and he warned the residents of Imvrildara of the coming of Treerazer and the devastation this demonic force would bring.

As Treerazer began to push out from his dominion in the Tanglebriar, the elves of Imvrildara stood defiantly in his path. Treerazer sent the nalfeshnee Echataxun to destroy the troublesome stronghold. Alendeil defeated Echataxun alone in single combat, calling on a miracle from Calistria herself to lock the demon perpetually in stone. Alendeil dedicated the centuries of his life to working against Treerazer, and his preparations ensured the Imvrildarai could stand against the demonic incursion.

When the migration of elves from Castrovel back to Golarion occurred in 2632 AR, the Imvrildarai assisted them in driving Treerazer and his forces back into the

Tanglebriar, though skirmishes and engagements with Treerazer's forces never reached the heights seen during the years just after his first arrival. These easy victories bred complacency within the priesthood, culminating in the appointment of High Priest Rekaereil Sandurei, a moderate archivist primarily concerned with the preservation of historic and religious texts.

In 4714 AR, several cambions caught Rekaereil outside of the temple in a well-coordinated assassination attempt and stole away with the high priest's body before anyone could come to his aid. Now, the Imvrildarai are on edge and anxiously awaiting an attack that is long overdue.

## ORGANIZATION

The priests of Imvrildara, collectively known as the Imvrildarai, are led by a high priest appointed by leaders of the Imvrildarai's two distinct branches, the Scions of Deceit and the Scions of Revenge. Below each head of the Scions are numerous elves serving as archivists, cooks, gardeners, and scribes, and filling other roles as needed.

## MEMBERSHIP AND RELATIONS

The current high priest of the Imvrildarai is Delerenai Ashwalker (see page 57), a militant-minded soldier and former head of the Scions of Revenge. The current head of the House of Revenge, Keshmarada (see page 57), is manipulating Delerenai into supporting her own ambitious push for power and influence within the faith.

The head of the Scions of Deceit is **Almeredei Songbreaker** (CN female elf bard 8), a clever cryptographer and expert at subterfuge and stealth. Almeredei was a close friend of the former high priest Rekaereil and sees the Imvrildarai as wardens of dangerous knowledge, rather than soldiers versed in esoteric lore. Almeredei is

so caught up in acclimating to her new position that she is woefully unaware of the threat that the head of the Scions of Revenge represents.

**Keshmarada** (CE female elf sorcerer 12) is an anomaly within the Imvrildarai. She was once an ally of the armies of Kyonin, a graceful and lethal warrior tasked with subverting the ranks of demons in the Tanglebriar from within by the Shin'Rakorath, a secretive elven paramilitary organization. Keshmarada became trapped in the Abyss during a conflict in the Tanglebriar nearly a century ago, and she spent decades struggling to win her way home.

After her return, Keshmarada sought out the Shin'Rakorath, demanding satisfaction for the suffering she endured. But with the passage of centuries, her name—and her sacrifice—had been forgotten. The Shin'Rakorath saw her as but another twisted abomination of the Tanglebriar and attempted to kill her. Swearing vengeance not only on the demons who stole decades of her life, but also on the elves who sent her into harm's way, Keshmarada wandered Kyonin for years before stumbling upon Imvrildara.

While she did not join the Imvrildarai as a member of the faith, Keshmarada found solace in the Imvrildarai's interpretation of her aspect of revenge. But the hollow in Keshmarada's warped soul could not be filled by kinship or faith—only by bringing suffering to her enemies. This wraith of a sorceress has manipulated the minds of Imvrildara's priests, slowly attaining power and influence within the organization. Keshmarada hopes to sway the organization into turning on the current regime of Kyonin—and by extension, the Shin'Rakorath—by painting them as unwilling to commit to a full offensive against Treerazer and thereby as accomplices to the horrors wrought by his presence.

Keshmarada's ultimate goal is not to lead the Imvrildarai directly, but to become the power behind the high priest and exact her revenge on all those who have wronged her.

## NOTABLE DENIZENS

The Imvrildarai include a wide range of priests of the Savored Sting, from alchemists to bards, clerics, and even antipaladins. The welcome an outsider receives is strongly dependent on the opinion of the Revered One, High Priestess Delerenai Ashwalker. For the moment, her interest in taking military action against Treerazer and his minions colors how she views any visitor. Those likely to support her politically or militarily, or who she feels she can readily convince to do so, are treated as valued guests.

| DELERENAI ASHWALKER | CR 11 |
|---|---|

**XP 12,800**

Female elf warpriest of Calistria 12 (*Pathfinder RPG Advanced Class Guide* 60)

CN Medium humanoid (elf)

**Init** +1; **Senses** low-light vision; Perception +5

### DEFENSE

**AC** 20, touch 12, flat-footed 18 (+7 armor, +1 Dex, +1 dodge, +1 natural)

**hp** 105 (12d8+48)

**Fort** +10, **Ref** +5, **Will** +11; +2 vs. enchantments

**Defensive Abilities** sacred armor (+2, 12 minutes/day); **Immune** sleep

### OFFENSE

**Speed** 30 ft.

**Melee** *+1 whip* +13/+8 (1d10+3 nonlethal)

**Special Attacks** blessings 9/day, channel positive energy 4/day (DC 19, 4d6), fervor 9/day (4d6), sacred weapon (+3 1d10, 12 rounds/day)

**Warpriest Spells Prepared** (CL 12th; concentration +15)

4th—*freedom of movement, persistent vigor*^ACG, *poison* (DC 17)

3rd—*dispel magic, invisibility purge, magic vestment, protection from energy, greater stunning barrier*^ACG (DC 16)

2nd—*delay poison, hold person* (DC 15), *instrument of agony*^UC, *lesser restoration, shatter* (DC 15), *silence* (DC 15)

1st—*divine favor, protection from law, remove fear, sanctuary* (DC 14), *shield of faith, sun metal*^UC

0 (at will)—*create water, detect magic, detect poison, guidance, light*

### STATISTICS

**Str** 14, **Dex** 13, **Con** 14, **Int** 10, **Wis** 16, **Cha** 12

**Base Atk** +9; **CMB** +11; **CMD** 23

**Feats** Combat Reflexes, Dodge, Greater Weapon of the Chosen^ACG, Improved Vital Strike, Improved Weapon of the Chosen^ACG, Improved Whip Mastery^UC, Toughness, Vital Strike, Weapon Focus (whip), Weapon of the Chosen^ACG, Whip Mastery^UC

**Skills** Heal +7, Knowledge (religion) +10, Perception +5, Sense Motive +14, Spellcraft +11 (+13 to identify magic item properties); **Racial Modifiers** +2 Perception, +2 Spellcraft to identify magic item properties

**Languages** Common, Elven, Gnome

**SQ** blessings (knowledge: lore keeper, monster lore, trickery: double, greater invisibility), elven magic

**Combat Gear** *potion of displacement, potion of fly, potion of invisibility, wand of cure light wounds;* **Other Gear** *+1 mithral breastplate, +1 whip, amulet of natural armor +1, belt of mighty constitution +2,* 299 gp

## GAZETTEER

Imvrildara is an overgrown monument to ages past, both showing signs of its millennia of use and proudly displaying proof of its durability even under the direst conditions. Dozens of trees bristle up from the perimeter of the temple, and three towers rise from a

inner sea temples

Sacred Spaces and Profane Places

Cathedral of Exquisite Agony

Cayden's Hall

First Colonial Bank of Sargava

High Temple of Pharasma

House of Dawn's Redemption

Imvrildara

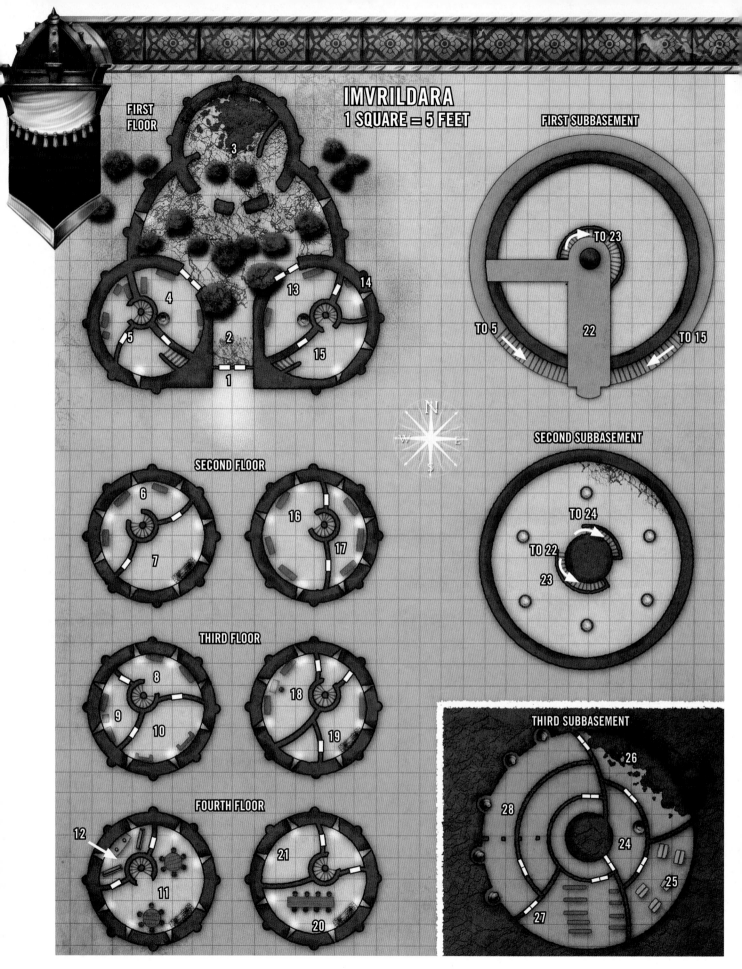

IMVRILDARA
1 SQUARE = 5 FEET

FIRST FLOOR

FIRST SUBBASEMENT

SECOND FLOOR

SECOND SUBBASEMENT

THIRD FLOOR

FOURTH FLOOR

THIRD SUBBASEMENT

mostly collapsed dome, with only a third of its total coverage remaining.

## 1. ENTRANCE (CR 9)

The main gates of Imvrildara are 15 feet tall and 10 feet wide, made of thick iron (hardness 10, hp 90, break DC 30).

**Creatures:** A pair of warmonger wasps living in elaborate and anarchistic hives in the high boughs of the pine attempts to slay intruders who attack members of the Imvrildarai or attempt to forcibly enter the temple.

| WARMONGER WASPS (2) | CR 7 |
|---|---|

**XP 3,200 each**

**hp** 85 each (*Pathfinder RPG Bestiary 5* 274)

## 2. COURTYARD (CR 10)

Under Imvrildara's crumbling dome, a small copse of pine trees grows unchecked. Moss-covered rubble from the collapsed dome and part of the Tower of Lust lies hidden among the tall grass. The gardens to either side of the walkway are now overgrown with flowering weeds.

The Scions of Revenge manage a number of wasp hives in the courtyard. These are of the same breed of honey-giving wasps as kept in the Pleasure Salon of Calistria in Absalom, and the honey the priests harvest from the hives is kept in the larder.

**Creatures:** The bones of roughly 50 priests are buried beneath the soft earth of the overgrown gardens. Six centuries ago, they willingly chose to be buried here and have their remains reanimated into a pair of powerful guecubus, who see all enemies of Imvrildara as worthy of their desire for revenge. Only overt acts against the temple or its walls draw the attention of the undead, which have not arisen in nearly 100 years, though the temple's Sacred One is able to name a target for the guecubus.

| GUECUBUS (2) | CR 8 |
|---|---|

**XP 4,800 each**

**hp** 104 each (*Pathfinder RPG Bestiary 3* 145)

## 3. THE TOWER OF LUST

Once used by the Scions of Lust, a now defunct order of the Imvrildarai, the Tower of Lust is little more than a broken ring of stone and rubble. In 3732 AR, when Treerazer's lieutenant Mokravud led an assault on the Fierani Forest, the temple of Imvrildara sat squarely in the glabrezu's path. The Imvrildarai defiantly held the temple for a week, even after a retriever under Mokravud's command tore through the temple's defenses and sundered the Tower of Lust.

The few surviving Scions of Lust departed the temple before plans for reconstruction could be considered. The tower became a monument, of sorts, to the dedication of Calistria's priests in holding their bastion of faith.

With the influence of the Scions of Lust gone, the temple gradually took on more militant tendencies and delved deeper into Calistria's aspects of deceit and revenge.

## 4. TOWER OF REVENGE FOYER (CR 8)

The Tower of Revenge's foyer prominently features a marble statue of Calistria standing over a fallen genderless figure that has been decapitated. Shelves in the room contain religious texts and historic texts regarding acts of revenge. A character consulting this library gains a +4 bonus on Knowledge (history) or (religion) checks regarding Kyonin and the worship of Calistria.

**Creature:** The victim lying at Calistria's feet in the room's impressive statue is in fact a cephalophore that is nearly impossible to distinguish from a typical statue (Perception DC 30). If the construct perceives a threat to the Tower of Revenge, it stands, picks up its head, and proceeds to protect the tower. It takes no actions to protect any area in Imvrildara outside this tower.

| CEPHALOPHORE | CR 8 |
|---|---|

**XP 4,800**

**hp** 96 (*Pathfinder RPG Bestiary 4* 27)

## 5. LANDING

A stained-glass window, depicting Calistria holding a knife in each hand with a third blade hovering point down above her head, overlooks the stairs to the basement. An adjacent study is used by the Scions of Revenge to keep track of demonic activity in the region and note the names of demons encountered but not slain, as well as those contained in the Stone Library (see page 61).

## 6. RECORDS (CR 6)

This room contains a modest collection of historical records regarding the Imvrildara.

**Creature:** Archivist Deneril is happy to discuss records with visitors but is likely to lie about any information desired unless a more powerful priest of Calistria indicates the information is needed for the protection of Imvrildara.

| DENERIL | CR 6 |
|---|---|

**XP 2,400**

Heretic (*Pathfinder RPG NPC Codex* 247)

**hp** 36

## 7. TRAINING ROOM (CR 9)

Anywhere from five to eight of the Scions of Revenge use this room as a sparring ground during daytime hours, practicing with whips and knives during this time. At night the hall is converted into communal living quarters using reed sleeping mats.

**Creature:** Master Jinen spends most of his time assisting in weapon drills and training exercises when he isn't

inner sea temples

Sacred Spaces and Profane Places

Cathedral of Exquisite Agony

Cayden's Hall

First Colonial Bank of Sargava

High Temple of Pharasma

House of Dawn's Redemption

Imvrildara

preoccupied by arguments with Keshmarada regarding the utilization of temple resources. He defends this room against any intruder who isn't a member of the Imvrildarai.

| JINEN | CR 9 |
|---|---|

**XP 6,400**

Dancing dervish (*Pathfinder RPG NPC Codex* 149)

**hp** 68

### 8. Reliquaries

Whenever members of the priesthood have died over the temple's history, a portion of their remains is interred in glass jars in this chamber. These remains are occasionally reviewed with *harvest knowledge* to glean information that might lead to taking vengeance for their death.

### 9. Delerenai's Quarters

Delerenai's personal quarters contain the skull of a particularly cruel babau, resting on a table between the shelves. She keeps the skull as a reminder of her late wife Esaril, who was the Imvrildarai's prior master of arms before perishing in an ambush 46 years ago.

### 10. Armory

Collections of weapons harvested from fallen demons, as well as those purchased from traders or donated to the temple, are kept here behind strong, locked doors. Jinen, the Imvrildarai's master-at-arms, is a lax caretaker of these armaments and spends little time in this room due to the painful memories it evokes of the previous master-at-arms.

### 11. Common Room

This spacious common room shared by all members of the Scions of Revenge used to be livelier, featuring music and song from the faithful during the day. Recent hardships and the death of High Priest Rekaereil have dampened the spirits of all.

### 12. Shrine of Revenge

An altar to Calistria flanked by a pair of simple wooden pews fills this small, dimly lit room. When it is an appropriate form of revenge, offerings of slain enemies' blood are placed atop the altar.

### 13. Tower of Deceit Foyer

A statue of Calistria, dressed in a gauzy robe with a strip of cloth held over her eyes, stands watch over the entrance to this sparsely decorated hall. Its shelves contain deceptively comprehensive religious texts penned by former members of the Scions of Deceit. Passages of Calistria's mythological history are contained within the parables and anecdotes, including some of the most detailed accounts of her participation in the battle with Rovagug in the Age Before Ages. In order to interpret these texts, readers must spend 8 hours studying the archive and succeed at both a DC 20 Knowledge (religion) check and a DC 25 Linguistics check. Failure on either of these checks indicates a false interpretation of the encoded knowledge. Succeeding at both of these checks grants readers a +8 bonus on Knowledge (history) and (religion) checks pertaining to Calistria when they use this library for research.

### 14. Study

This small study is features low-set tables with padded reed mats for seats. A handful of priests typically study scripture here and make copies of old or damaged texts.

### 15. Landing (CR 7)

Stairs here connect to the basement of the Imvrildara.

**Creature:** This stairway is protected by a soulbound mannequin disguised as a male priest of Calistria carrying a book and an inkwell. It prefers to convince visitors it is a living elven priest, but it won't actually leave this room other than to protect the Tower of Deceit.

| SOULBOUND MANNEQUIN | CR 7 |
|---|---|

**XP 3,200**

**hp** 85 (*Pathfinder RPG Bestiary 4* 248)

### 16. Common Room

Priests use this chamber for personal recreation during daytime hours and convert them at night into a barracks of sorts where the Scions of Deceit share sleeping space.

### 17. Ocularum

Three armoires line the walls of this chamber, each containing a pair of full-length mirrors. Priests use this chamber to practice arts of deception, from practical disguises to illusion magic. The middle cabinet is locked (Disable Device DC 30) and contains a *mirror of opposition* used only by permission of Almeredei.

### 18. Scrivening Study

Tall oaken shelves of scrolls dominate this chamber, flanking a comparatively small writing desk. This room is used exclusively to pen magical scrolls.

### 19. Kitchen

Priests from both sects split shifts preparing meals here and often use this time to gossip with one another. The adjoining larder is never sufficiently stocked, and orders for spices and vegetables that can't be procured in the Fierani Forest are frequently tacked to the door.

### 20. Great Hall

This room takes up half of the tower's top floor. Meetings among the upper echelons of the Scions of

Deceit are held here at the long, oaken table, along with shared meals and other official gatherings.

## 21. ALMEREDEI'S CHAMBERS (CR 8)

The personal quarters of Almeredei Songbreaker (see page 56) contain 160 years of collected books and baubles. An *iron flask* sitting on her desk contains the nabasu demon Anochnodan. Almeredei sees her prisoner more as a keepsake, but she occasionally plumbs the demon's experiences with *harvest knowledge* (see page 62).

## 22. SANCTUARY

This shrine comprises a pair of open platforms leading from the west and south walls, respectively, out to the middle of an open, circular space. A spiral staircase descends the central column, while a ramp climbs the exterior wall. A statue of Calistria stands atop the column. The statue is carved from white marble and is perpetually soaked in blood that runs in a streak down Calistria's body. The wall formed by the spiral stair behind her contains the skulls of the departed faithful.

## 23. ABYSSAL CODICES (CR 11)

Thousands of texts detailing artifacts, entities, and locations of the Abyss are held here. The library is lit by six iron braziers containing *continual flame*. Poring through the texts grants those who research here a +8 bonus on all Knowledge checks pertaining to the Abyss, its inhabitants, or their creations after 24 hours of study.

**Creatures:** A group of four invisible stalkers attack any intruders not escorted by Delerenai.

| INVISIBLE STALKERS (4) | CR 7 |
|---|---|

**XP 3,200 each**

**hp** 80 each (*Pathfinder RPG Bestiary* 181)

## 24. BONE SHRINE

The outer wall of this chamber is the Archive of the Slain, a collection of skulls belonging to ancient enemies of the Calistrian faith, most of which served orders long since lost to time.

## 25. TREASURY

Behind a locked iron door (Disable Device DC 35) lies Imvrildara's treasury. Monetary wealth is fleeting here, with barely enough currency to maintain the temple. However, the treasury is also an archive of collected demonic ephemera, including schematics for constructs such as warmonger wasps (see page 59).

## 26. COLLAPSED ARCHIVE

This chamber once held the books in the Abyssal Codices, but an attempt by demonic forces to breach the vault by burrowing into the basement led to a structural collapse.

## 27. MEDITATION CHAMBER

Filled with well-appointed benches and silk pillows, this chamber is used by senior priests as a place to meditate on information gained from the Stone Library (area **28**).

## 28. STONE LIBRARY

Imvrildara's greatest secret is the Stone Library, where the petrified forms of five demons trapped by *flesh to stone* spells grant access to untold Abyssal knowledge. These demons—Celedranus, a nabasu; Echataxun, a nalfeshnee; Haldrezenei, a succubus; Jadramarcha, a vrock; and Nerchius, a hezrou—each led a failed assault on Imvrildara. Now these demons serve as repositories of information for the priesthood, accessed through the *harvest knowledge* spell.

inner sea temples

Sacred Spaces and Profane Places

Cathedral of Exquisite Agony

Cayden's Hall

First Colonial Bank of Sargava

High Temple of Pharasma

House of Dawn's Redemption

Imvrildara

DELERENAI ASHWALKER

## CALISTRIAN MAGIC

The Imvrildarai favor the following magic items and spells.

### CALISTRIAN MAGIC ITEMS

The Imvrildarai use the following magic items to set up spectacular acts of trickery or vengeance.

| ELIXIR OF EMULATION | | PRICE 4,000 GP |
|---|---|---|
| **SLOT** none | **CL** 9th | **WEIGHT** — |
| **AURA** moderate transmutation | | |

A drinker must add hair, skin, fur, blood, or nail clippings of a single creature to this elixir before drinking it, or it is expended uselessly. Once appropriate material has been added, the elixir retains potency for 24 hours, after which it becomes an inert, valueless liquid. If drunk while potent, the elixir functions as *alter self*, allowing the drinker to assume the shape of the donor creature, which must be a living, corporeal, Small or Medium creature. In addition, the elixir aids the drinker in duplicating the mannerisms of the donor creature, granting her a +20 bonus on Disguise checks to pass herself off as that creature and eliminating the penalty for masquerading as a different gender, race, or age. Once during the elixir's duration, the drinker can try to learn information known by the donor creature at the time its material was harvested, as if she had cast *harvest knowledge* (see below). An *elixir of emulation* lasts 2d6+12 hours.

| CONSTRUCTION REQUIREMENTS | COST 2,000 GP |
|---|---|

Craft Wondrous Item, *detect thoughts*, *polymorph*

| HATEFUL STING | | PRICE 60,302 GP |
|---|---|---|
| **SLOT** none | **CL** 15th | **WEIGHT** 1 lb. |
| **AURA** strong transmutation | | |

This *+1 dancing dagger* can attack foes up to 60 feet from the activating character, and takes the form of a rat-sized metal wasp when the *dancing* special ability is in use. It can store up to 4 doses of poison in its hilt. While dancing, if it does not currently have poison applied to it, it automatically applies 1 dose of stored poison (if any is currently stored) to itself before the first attack it makes each round. The *hateful sting* can envenom itself only when dancing. Removing the poison from the hilt to apply to the blade manually takes a full-round action.

| CONSTRUCTION REQUIREMENTS | COST 30,302 GP |
|---|---|

Craft Magic Arms and Armor, *animate objects*, *summon swarm*

### CALISTRIAN SPELLS

These spells are known by few outside the Imvrildarai, but other Calistrian priests and spellcasters can use them.

#### BETRAYING STING

**School** evocation; **Level** cleric 6, occultist 6, psychic 6, shaman 6, witch 6

**Casting Time** 1 standard action

**Components** V

**Range** long (400 ft. + 40 ft./level)

**Target** one creature

**Duration** instantaneous

**Saving Throw** Will partial; **Spell Resistance** yes

You unleash divine power to smite those who wrongly trusted you. The power takes the form of a yellow-and-black bolt of energy that makes the sound of a thousand angry, swarming wasps. This spell affects only creatures that have an attitude toward you of indifferent, friendly, or helpful. The spell deals 1d8 points of damage per 2 caster levels you have.

#### HARVEST KNOWLEDGE

**School** divination [mind-affecting]; **Level** alchemist 4, antipaladin 4, bard 4, inquisitor 4, mesmerist 4, psychic 4, sorcerer/wizard 4, witch 4

**Casting Time** 1 standard action

**Components** V, S, M (a piece of lodestone)

**Range** touch (see text)

**Target** one creature or object; see text

**Duration** concentration, up to 1 minute/level

**Saving Throw** Will negates; see text; **Spell Resistance** no

You touch a creature and temporarily absorb its knowledge for yourself. If the target fails its saving throw, you can sort through its lore and memories. You can retrieve one answer to a specific question per minute, as through sifting through the creature's surface thoughts with *detect thoughts*. Alternatively, you can tap into the target's learned experiences and attempt one Knowledge check in a skill in which the target has at least 1 rank, using the target's total skill modifier. Each Knowledge check requires 1 minute and allows the target another Will save to resist the effect. If the target successfully resists, the spell does not end, but you are unable to attempt another Knowledge check for that skill using this spell. You can also use this spell against targets trapped in magic items or spells that hold their bodies or souls, such as an *iron flask* or the spell *trap the soul*, by touching the associated receptacle.

#### INCESSANT BUZZING

**School** illusion (figment); **Level** antipaladin 1, bard 1, psychic 1, shaman 1, sorcerer/wizard 1, witch 1

**Casting Time** 1 standard action

**Components** V, S, M/DF (insect wing)

**Range** medium (100 ft. +10 ft./level)

**Effect** 10-ft.-diameter sphere

**Duration** 1 round/level

**Saving Throw** Will negates; **Spell Resistance** yes

You summon an illusory swarm of angry wasps that fills a 10-foot-diameter sphere. You can summon it so that it shares an area with other creatures, and you can move it up to 40 feet each round as a move action. Creatures caught inside the swarm's area of effect cannot use skills that require patience or concentration. Additionally, spellcasters within the area must succeed at a caster level check (DC =

20 + level of spell to be cast) in order to cast spells. On a failed caster level check, the spell is lost. While the buzzing is unpleasant, it is not so loud as to drown out other noises or make communication difficult.

## PAINFUL REVELATION

**School** abjuration [mind-affecting, pain<sup>UM</sup>]; **Level** antipaladin 2, bard 2, mesmerist 2, psychic 2, sorcerer/wizard 2

**Casting Time** 1 standard action

**Components** V, S

**Range** close (25 ft. + 5 ft./2 levels)

**Target** one ongoing illusion effect

**Duration** 1 hour/level or until discharged

**Saving Throw** Will partial; **Spell Resistance** no

You augment an ongoing illusion effect to strike out painfully at creatures that see through it. When a creature successfully disbelieves an illusion that is the target of *painful revelation*, it takes 1d6 points of nonlethal damage for every 2 caster levels you have (maximum 10d6) and is staggered for 1d4 rounds. A successful Will save reduces the nonlethal damage by half and negates the staggered effect. Once *painful revelation* has been triggered, the spell ends.

However, creatures under the effect of spells such as *true seeing* that automatically pierce illusions are not subject to this effect.

## PILLOW TALK

**School** enchantment (compulsion) [language-dependent, mind-affecting]; **Level** bard 3, inquisitor 3, mesmerist 3, psychic 3, sorcerer/wizard 3, witch 3

**Casting Time** 10 minutes

**Components** S

**Range** touch

**Target** sleeping, living creature touched

**Duration** 1 minute/level

**Saving Throw** Will negates; see text; **Spell Resistance** yes

This spell can be cast only on a sleeping creature, which must be present for the full duration of the casting time. You grant the semblance of wakefulness to the target, allowing it to answer questions. You can ask one question per 2 caster levels. The target's knowledge is limited to what it normally knows, including the languages it speaks. Answers are brief, cryptic, or repetitive, especially if the creature would have opposed you when awake. If the target succeeds at a Will save, it awakens (unless some force is

preventing it from being awake, such as magic or drugs), and it remains aware of the first question you asked. If the target has been subject to *pillow talk* within the past week, the new spell fails. While your questions don't otherwise wake the target, this spell does nothing to prevent other sounds or stimulus from waking the target. A target who sleeps through the spellcasting and duration of the spell has no memory of it taking place, but a target who awakens before the spell ends remembers every question asked and what answers it gave.

## REVEAL SECRETS

**School** enchantment (compulsion) [language-dependent, mind-affecting]; **Level** bard 1, inquisitor 1, mesmerist 1, psychic 1, sorcerer/wizard 1, witch 1

**Casting Time** 1 standard action

**Components** V, S, M (a drop of alcoholic liquid)

**Range** touch

**Target** creature touched

**Duration** 1 round

**Saving Throw** Will negates; **Spell Resistance** yes

When you cast this spell, you ask the target whether it has a secret about a specific topic that can be described in 10 words or fewer. This can concern a person, place, or thing (such as a town's mayor, the ring worn by a traveling merchant, or the bridge spanning a nearby river) or an easily distinguished event (such as a historic battle or a recent rash of disappearances). If the target knows a secret about the topic (information it believes isn't common knowledge and which it would not normally tell you), it states it has a secret. The target doesn't mention anything about the secret and doesn't remember telling you it has a secret. If the target succeeds at its saving throw, it isn't compelled to reveal whether it knows a secret and is aware that you asked.

### NEW SPELLS

Worshipers of Calistria gain access to the new spells as noted below.

**Betraying Sting**: bard 6
**Harvest Knowledge**: cleric 4, ranger 4
**Incessant Buzzing**: cleric 1
**Painful Revelation**: cleric 2, witch 2
**Pillow Talk**: antipaladin 3, cleric 3
**Reveal Secrets**: antipaladin 1, cleric 1